Karen Wikholm

International Perspecti[ves on]
Selected p[apers]
Supporting Deaf Peopl[e]

Edited by Judith Mole

Direct Learn Services Ltd.

Published by Direct Learn Services Ltd., The Limes, Norbury, Shropshire, United Kingdom

www.directlearn.co.uk

© Direct Learn Services Ltd. 2009

This book is subject to copyright laws. No reproduction or transmission, in part or in whole, is permitted without the written permission of the publishers. Any unauthorised copying, reproduction, transmission, or distribution of this book is strictly prohibited.

ISBN 978-1-905938-05-6

Table of contents

Table of contents 3

Introduction 5

A model of learning within an interpreted K-12 educational setting by Brenda Schick 6

    Summary of the conference discussion 25

Giving Voice: Sign to Voice Interpreting for Hearing Consumers in K-12 settings in the United States, by Richard Brumberg 28

    Appendix - Transcriptions of Selected Video Captures 40
    Summary of the conference discussion 45

Language and Learning by Deaf Students by Loes Wauters, Marc Marschark, Patricia Sapere and Carol Convertino 51

    Summary of the conference discussion 63

Boundary Issues in Educational Interpreting: Where do You Draw the Line? by Richard Brumberg 69

    Summary of the conference discussion 80

Education of the Deaf: Mediated by Interpreters by Patricia Lessard 84

    Appendix A: Non Manual Signals 106
    Appendix B: State required minimal EIPA standards 107
    Appendix C: CI and CT (Generalist) Rating Scales 111
    Appendix D: RID Certification Requirements 113
    Summary of the conference discussion 115

Practical Application of the Demand Control Schema with an Educational Interpreter: A Case Study by Kendra Keller 119

Educational Interpreting: Multiple Perspectives on our Work From Deaf students, teachers, administrators and parents, by Debra Russell and Jane McLeod 140

    Summary of the conference discussion 159

Ten years of bilingual deaf education in Norway – where are we? by Arnfinn Muruvik Vonen 164

    Summary of the conference discussion 170

Index 176

Introduction

The first Supporting Deaf People online conference was held in 2001. There have been six such conferences now, and they have become an annual event. Originally the conferences were set up for two purposes:

- To provide high quality, low cost staff development for those people who are least likely to be provided with training and professional development within organisations, e.g. freelance interpreters, sessional educational interpreters (in the UK, Communication Support Workers) and deaf people.

- To provide an international platform for discussion on topics related to deafness and supporting deaf people.

Over the six conferences there have been over hundreds of delegates from 25 countries, spread over five continents.

The proceedings cannot begin to reproduce the whole online conference experience (the exciting atmosphere, meeting people online from all over the world, the sharing of experience and resources) although a summary of discussions is provided here.

Selected other papers from the conferences are available in the *International Perspectives on Interpreting - Selected Proceedings of the Supporting Deaf People online conferences 2001 - 2005* and *International Perspectives on Language Support - Selected Proceedings of the Supporting Deaf People online conferences 2001 – 2005* ebooks and paperbacks; certain other papers from these conferences can be downloaded free of charge from http://www.deafshop.co.uk/ashop/catalogue.php

A special thank you to all the conference delegates from the 2006 and 2008 SDP conferences whose postings have contributed to the summaries.

A model of learning within an interpreted K-12 educational setting
by Brenda Schick

While we know that students who are deaf or hard of hearing (d/hh) can learn through an interpreted education, there is considerable variability among children (Kurz, 2004) and college students (Marschark et al., 2004, 2005). We know that at least some d/hh students learn less through interpretation, but research also shows that they may bring less content knowledge to the classroom as well (Marschark et al., 2004, 2005). Much of the research and analysis regarding educational access with an interpreter has focused on the interpreter's *interpreting* skills, either directly (Schick et al., 1999, 2006) or indirectly (e.g., Jones et al., 1997) or the teacher's discourse (Jones, 2004; Winston, 2004). However, kindergarten through twelfth grade classrooms (K-12) are complex learning environments (in the U.S., children begin formal schooling by kindergarten, or age 6) and complete high school, or 12th grade, about age 18. In order to better understand how children might learn in an interpreted education, we need a framework or model for the constellation of factors that may impact the student's ability to learn and achieve academic success. An overview of a model of learning through an interpreter is shown in Figure 1 and the purpose of this paper is to explore these factors and what we know about them. See Schick (in press) for a more in depth discussion of this model.

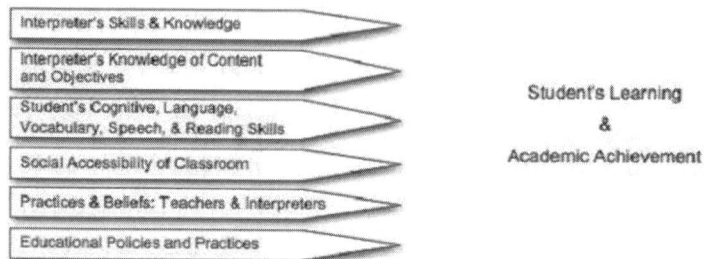

Figure 1. Model of factors that likely affect a student's learning in an interpreted education.

Interpreter's Skills and Knowledge related to Interpreting

The language, world knowledge, and cognitive skills that underlie the process of interpretation are complex and there are models that focus on just this component (Cokely, 1992; Dean & Pollard, 2005; Napier, 2004; Roy, 2000; Seleskovitch, 1992; Setton, 1999; Witter-Merithew & Johnson, 2005). While it seems obvious that an interpreter's skills and knowledge related to interpreting would affect student learning, few investigations have explored this relationship. Research on working educational interpreters in the U.S. shows that many do not have language and interpreting skills that are commonly considered as minimum standards in the U.S.. Research using the Educational Interpreter Performance Assessment (Schick, Williams, & Bolster, 1999; Schick, Williams, & Kupermintz, 2006) shows that 45% of more than 2,000 interpreters did not have sufficient interpreting skills to be in a classroom. Other research has shown that deaf adults have considerable difficulty learning elementary-school content when learning through an educational interpreter; learning about 40% of the content while hearing people learned 99% of the content (Langer, 2006; Langer & Schick, in preparation).

Nearly all models of interpreting include significant aspects related to the interpreter's cognitive and metacognitive skills that impact critical analysis, language analysis, conceptualisation, memory, pragmatic analysis, and other fundamental skills involved in interpretation. We see some effects of the interpreter's metacognition at work in their omissions of information while interpreting text. Napier (2004) showed that interpreters are often aware of their omissions of content during interpreting, and that many omissions were strategic, where the interpreter reported making a conscious decision to omit something to enhance the effectiveness of the interpretation. There were also many omissions that the interpreter consciously made because their own lack of understanding or sign vocabulary knowledge. In short, many educational interpreters lack sufficient interpreting skills and this must affect the quality of their interpreting product.

Interpreters' Knowledge of Educational Systems, Class Content, and Learning

Qualifications for interpreters involve more than fluency in two languages. There is a large amount of foundational knowledge that underlies working as a related service provider in an educational setting with a developing student (La Bue, 1998; Roy, 2000; Schick, 2004; Seal, 2004; Shroyer & Compton, 1994; Stewart, Schein, & Cartwright, 2004). However, interpreter education programs have mostly focused on the knowledge required to work with adults (see Schick, in press). Schick (2005, 2007) developed a basic written test for educational interpreters, the EIPA Written Test. The test assesses knowledge in 10 domains related to the K-12 setting including child development, professional practices, language and cognitive development, interpreting, educational practices, tutoring, and literacy. Results from a large sample of educational interpreters (n = 551) showed that interpreters vary in their knowledge of content related to interpreting as well as basic English skills; the overall average was 83 % correct ($SD = 10.15$).

Because many d/hh children are delayed in language and cognitive skills, an educational interpreter may need to scaffold the student's learning by modifying content, repeating key concepts, emphasising new vocabulary, etc. It seems essential that the educational interpreter understand the child from a developmental and educational perspective, not just understand the process of interpretation. Given that the interpreter can never realistically convey all classroom communication, it is critical that the interpreter be able to make informed decisions about the changes and omissions. As we know from Napier's work (2004), interpreters are altering the teacher's talk in conscious ways. When the interpreter does not understand the educational process, decisions will still be made, but they may not facilitate the teacher's educational outcomes, or they may not be in the child's best educational interests. While models of adult-to-adult interpreting include significant cognitive components, they are more about message analysis than thinking of the learning needs of the adult consumer or the teacher's educational goals.

For the educational interpreter, the interpreting process would also include metacognitive thinking about the student's skills, goals, as well as thinking about how to best represent the information via translation. For interpreters who work with students with functional speech communication skills, interpreting may also involve thinking about when and what to interpret, in order to allow the student to communicate using speech as much as possible.

We see the likely effect of this in research conducted by Langer (2007), who showed that both expert adult community interpreters and a wide range of educational interpreters were less likely to convey the teacher's talk about beliefs and attitudes than talk about word definitions, semantic categorisation, and directions. This is probably not due to the skills of the interpreters; rather it is more likely a reflection of the interpreter's beliefs about the importance of this type of talk to student learning. As Langer puts it, talk about beliefs and attitudes were communicated as facts or were simply omitted as if non-essential to the communication. However, the student's understanding of the beliefs and attitudes of teachers and peers is essential to the learning process, not extraneous communication (Astington & Pelletier, 1996, 2005; Sodian, Zaitchik, & Carey, 1991; Wellman & Lagatutta, 2005), and may also underlie important social skills (Lalonde & Chandler, 1995; Leekam, 1991; Yuill & Perner, 1987).

In summary, the interpreter's understanding of educational systems and practices, of the teacher's goals and objectives, and of the student's abilities and IEP goals would provide the interpreter with the context and information to guide how they make decisions while interpreting. We know that there are conscious decisions being made that result in altered communication, but we have no idea whether the classroom teacher or the educational team would agree with the interpreter's decisions and the extent to which their decisions are driven by sound educational judgment.

Students' Skills: Cognition, Language, Vocabulary, Speech, and Reading Skills

It seems logical that the d/hh student's skills may mediate or moderate learning in an interpreted education, but we actually know very little about how school-age children with hearing loss learn in real classrooms. We know d/hh children with hearing parents typically enter school with significant language and vocabulary delays, compared with their hearing peers, even in recent studies with children with cochlear implants (Connor & Zwolan, 2004; Geers, 2003; Padden & Ramsey, 2000; Traxler, 2000). They often do not have the depth and breadth of conceptual knowledge, problem-solving skills, and cognitive organisation that their hearing peers demonstrate (Marschark, 2003).

There is some research that looks at how student factors influence learning in an interpreted education in d/hh college students. Marschark and his colleagues (2005) examined learning in d/hh college students in an interpreted condition and how it related to background variables. For their 105 d/hh participants, the results showed that none of the student variables accounted for differences, including reading level, degree or age of onset of hearing loss, parental hearing status, use of assistive listening devices, or the age at which Sign Language was learned. Marschark and his colleagues have found similar results in other studies looking for factors that were predictive of comprehension (Marschark et al., 2004, 2006) – basically the factors that we think are important are not. However, their participants were successfully matriculated at a university. It is impossible to generalise these results to K-12 students with a greater range of skills.

Kurz (2004) studied how well deaf children, with deaf parents and hearing parents, learned via direct versus interpreted communication (n = 19). She found that d/hh children with deaf families learned more through some interpreted lectures than their peers with hearing parents. This implies that better language skills results in better learning. There are numerous other differences between these two groups of children. It is an important but unanswered question about how delayed a student can be in these skill domains and still have sufficient "horsepower" to learn in an interpreted educational setting, particularly in classes with abstract concept and vocabulary.

Delays in cognition, language, and vocabulary may moderate learning for any child in any classroom, but their effects might be amplified for deaf children for several reasons. An interpreted education seems to place additional demands on cognitive processing (Schick, 2004). The student must coordinate visual attention between the interpreter and other visual information in the classroom, which means that the d/hh student likely receives less information than the hearing students (Winston, 2004). The d/hh student also must figure out who is speaking in the classroom in order to make sense of the message (Schick, 2004), a requirement that is challenging to represent for many interpreters (Schick et al., 2006). For their part, educational interpreters are typically second-language learners, so the student must deal with a variety of accents and errors. As we know, the interpretation is likely to be a less rich and complex version of the teacher's communication in addition to being riddled with distortions, errors, and omissions (Langer, 2007), which make learning more challenging. The d/hh student must contend with interpreted communication that is not in synchronisation with what the hearing teacher and peers are doing, pointing, and looking (Winston, 2004). This short list of increased demands on cognitive resources is clearly incomplete; we really do not know all the factors that may be involved.

Marschark (2003), in a summary of what we know about cognitive skills in d/hh students, concluded that they often have less efficient cognitive processing and retrieval strategies and they are more variable in the content and organisation of their cognitive system, all of which affect learning in the best of situations. A less robust cognitive system combined with the increased processing demands from learning through an interpreter may predict large differences in learning in d/hh students and their hearing peers within the same classroom environment. Delays in language and vocabulary may further moderate learning, especially because the teacher talk and learning objectives are scaffolded for students who are linguistically more mature.

Finally, the students' understanding of the interpreting process and their role in this process is likely to affect how effectively the student is able to learn in an interpreted classroom. For example, a student who understands that it is appropriate to ask the interpreter to slow down or clarify a concept, may be able to work with the interpreter and the classroom teacher to ensure better interpretation. However, this would require sophisticated metacognition, planning, and comprehension monitoring on the part of the student in order to manage communication and think about what would improve it. It also would require that schools teach students about their rights as a consumer, which is probably a questionable assumption.

Social Accessibility of the Classroom

Classrooms are complex social environments, and their social organisation is quite different than that of family interaction (Cazden, 2001; Hertz-Lazarowitz, 1992; Rogoff, 1990; Sharan, 1990). Many classrooms are highly interactive, with the locus of learning in cooperative group activities in addition to teacher-centered instruction. In addition to the positive effects of working with peers, there seems to be particular advantages for interaction and cooperative work with friends (Buklowski, Newcomb, & Hartup, 1996; Hartup, 1996a, 1996b; Ladd, 1990; Newcomb & Bagwell, 1996). The issues of cooperative learning and developing friendships can be problematic within an interpreted education. First, d/hh students may not have the maturity in social cognition skills that their hearing peers have. Research shows us that d/hh children tend to be significantly delayed in fundamental aspects of social cognition, specifically *theory of mind* skills as measured with false belief tasks (see Peterson, 2004; Schick, de Villiers, de Villiers, & Hoffmeister, 2007). Given these delays, it might be more difficult for some d/hh students to interpret the intentions of others, regardless of whether an interpreter is used.

However, accessing the social culture of the classroom may be particularly different in an interpreted education. The d/hh student may see all classroom communication through a single individual, creating a social barrier between peers and the teacher. Both d/hh children and adults report being left out, feeling socially isolated, with significant difficulties connecting with individuals other than the interpreter (Foster, 1988, 1989; Kurz & Langer, 2004; Mertens, 1991; Ramsey, 1997; Shaw & Jamieson, 1997).

The reduced information about the intentions of teachers and peers might also affect how the d/hh student views the teacher's goals in terms of learning (Astington & Pelletier, 2005; Frye & Ziv, 2005). As Richardson (in press) points out, d/hh students may view learning as memorization of facts, which may be in part due to being educated through an interpreter who views his or her role as a conduit, reproducing in a literal way what the teacher says.

There is evidence that the quality of interactions that d/hh students have with teachers and peers is affected by an interpreted education (Kurz & Langer, 2004; Lang, Stinson, Kavanaugh, Liu, & Basile, 1998; Ramsey, 1997). Kurz and Langer (2004) interviewed 20 d/hh K – 12 students about their beliefs and understanding of an interpreted education. Many of the students commented about issues related to social accessibility. For example, some students preferred a teacher's lecture to group discussions, because of difficulties interpreting discussions. Many students said that they participated less frequently in an interpreted class than in a class with direct communication. Some students expressed concerns about their confidence in the quality of the interpretation, which was an obstacle to participation.

Finally, it is important to note that interpreting a distributed conversation, such as in a classroom discussion, is more difficult than interpreting a monologue lecture (Winston, 2004). Research using the EIPA has shown that educational interpreters have difficulty representing who is speaking; that resulting in an interpretation that makes it seem like a single speaker is talking. Even when the interpreter is able to signal a speaker shift, the interpreter may not fully identify the individual, but just note that it was not the teacher. Given this, the student may not know that peers are making significant contributions and may not have access to which peer made which comment, which provides rich information about personalities and skills of others.

Educational Practices and Beliefs of the Teachers and Interpreters

A major aspect affecting learning relates to the professional practices of the educational team, including the classroom teacher and interpreter. Because educational interpreting is an emerging profession, standards of practice are not well-defined or established (Antia & Kreimeyer, 2001; Bolster, 2005; Seal, 1998, 2000). Many of the standards of practice for interpreting for adults are problematic in a K–12 setting, which has legal obligations not present in adult interpreting, and many practices do not seem to be in the best interest of a developing child. In many instances, educational interpreters are expected to transfer principles such as confidentiality and right to autonomy into a K-12 setting, resulting in conflicts in roles and responsibilities (Scheibe & Hoza, 1986; Seal, 2004; Stedt, 1992; Witter-Merithew & Dirst, 1982; Zawolkow, & DeFiore, 1986).

There is a great deal of controversy in the field about how engaged or involved the educational interpreter should be in the education of a d/hh student, other than providing a faithful rendition of the classroom communication (Antia & Kreimeyer, 2001; Stewart & Kluwin, 1996), although some researchers consider this neutrality to be impossible (Janzen & Shaffer, in press; Turner, 2005). For example, many interpreters believe that if the student appears to have difficulty understanding the interpreted message, it is not their responsibility to inform the teacher; rather it is the teacher's responsibility to find out. In their view, informing the teacher would be violating what they see as the child's right to confidentiality (Humphrey & Alcorn, 1994; Scheibe & Hoza, 1986), which seems to trump the child's right to an accessible and fair education.

Confusions also exist among classroom teachers and educational teams about the role and responsibilities of the educational interpreter. In a survey by Antia and Kreimeyer (2001), classroom teachers reported that they preferred a full-participant role for the interpreter, while the special educators and administrators preferred a more restricted model of interpreting, where the interpreter provides a translation of the communication but all other responsibilities belong to the classroom teacher. Bolster (2005) reported that of 65 educational interpreters who had completed an educational interpreting certificate program, only 57 % were invited to the educational meetings even though a thorough understanding of the student's educational goals seems essential to decision-making about interpreting. In a different survey of 59 general education teachers who work with educational interpreters, only 54 % reported that they discussed the issue of the roles and responsibilities of the educational interpreter (Beaver, Hayes, & Luetke-Stahlman, 1995). While educational interpreting is a widespread practice, it is clear that little attention has been given to the dynamics of the educational team.

The teacher's discourse and teaching style can influence the quality of interpretation. The teacher's management of the classroom discourse also affects how accessible a classroom is when interpreted. Winston (2004) analysed teachers' lectures, predicting how accurately it could be interpreted. She identified elements of teacher's style of communication that would directly impact the quality of the interpretation, such as the teachers' pacing, the extent to which the teacher is explicit and redundant, management of turn-taking, and whether the class used lecture rather than discussion-type lessons.

In summary, there are many aspects of educational practice and belief that affect how the interpreter works, either as a member of the educational team or as a communication conduit, which in turn may affect student learning. Part of the conflicts in roles that educational interpreters have is grounded in trying to apply a model of interpreting that was developed for adult consumers, who are independent and autonomous, to an educational setting where the educational team has a legal obligation to maximise education.

Policies and regulations

In the U.S., many states have established minimum skill standards for educational interpreters. However, the concept of standards, policies, and/or regulations is more complex than simply establishing a minimum skill level in interpreting skills. The quality of access in the classroom is also dependent on the interpreter's knowledge of the interpreting process, educational practices, the student's Individualised Education Program (IEP), the teacher's goals and objectives, as well as many other aspects of education. Nearly all states have focused mostly on the skills component and little on the knowledge component. The vast majority do not have degree requirements beyond the high school level.

Summary and Implications

Gaining access to a regular education classroom through an educational interpreter is a complex cognitive process with many interrelated factors. This paper attempts to provide an overview of the range of skills and factors that would influence how much and how well a child would learn within an interpreted education. There are good reasons why many people focus on the interpreter's skills in interpreting, because many individuals do not have what is considered minimum performance skills. However, there are many other domains of practice and skill that may mediate and moderate learning in an interpreted education.

It is obvious from reviewing the research related to learning within an interpreted K-12 setting that there is little empirical evidence to guide us when making decisions about individual students and their needs. While educational interpreting is a widespread practice, there is little data to help educational teams determine best practices. Most of what we do know focuses on college students and other adults, typically with interpreters that have been selected because of their high level of interpreting skills. We need research on K-12 students, with their broader range of skills and developmental needs, in order to ensure educational access, with information about how the interpreter's skills affect the quality of interpretation.

There are positive aspects to this complexity of factors, in that they provide multiple avenues that we can pursue to improve access in an interpreted education. Providing the interpreters with access to educational team meetings, the student's educational goals, and teacher manuals for textbooks may help the interpreter make better choices about how to prioritise competing needs. Similarly, an interpreter may provide the classroom teacher with information about what discourse and management styles facilitate interpretation. This model provides direction for a multi-pronged approach in improving our ability to ensure access within an interpreted education.

It is easy to view what we know about interpreted education and the challenges it brings to learning as a widespread indictment against the practice, however that seems unfair and perhaps unrealistic. There is evidence that students can learn through an interpreted education. Furthermore, choosing a school placement for a student is complex, and families and educational programs must weigh a variety of factors, often concluding that there is no ideal option. The d/hh students who were interviewed by Kurz and Langer (2004) seemed aware of the compromises inherent in an interpreted education. Furthermore, much of what is written about the relative pros and cons often assumes that the d/hh student cannot use spoken communication, and the student's skills are severely delayed. In reality, only about 9 % of children have a severe or profound hearing loss (Blanchfield, Feldman, & Dunbar, 2001). It is highly likely that in the future many more students will have some degree of functional skills in spoken communication and that language and literacy outcomes might well improve. Even with amplification (both hearing aids and cochlear implants), the noisy acoustic environments that are typical of K–12 classrooms pose serious listening challenges. We may likely see an increase in the number of families that choose to scaffold their child's learning environment with an educational interpreter, regardless of their ability to use spoken communication in some situations.

Acknowledgement

Preparation of this paper was supported in part by a grant from the U.S. Department of Education, Office of Special Education Programs, Programs of National Significance (H325 N010013).

References

Antia, S. & Kreimeyer, K. (2001). The role of interpreters in inclusive classrooms. *American Annals of the Deaf, 146*, 355-365.

Astington, J. W., & Pelletier, J. (1996). The language of the mind: Its role in teaching and learning. In D. Olson & N. Torrance (Eds.), *Handbook of education and human development: New models of learning, teaching, and schooling* (pp. 593 - 619). Cambridge, UK: Blackwell Press.

Astington, J. W. & Pelletier, J. (2005). Theory of mind, language, and learning in the early years: Developmental origins of school readiness. In B. D. Homer & C. Tamis-Lemonda (Eds.), *The development of social cognition and communication* (pp. 205-230). Hillsdale, NJ: Erlbaum.

Beaver, D.L., Hayes, P.L., & Luetke-Stahlman, B. (1995). In-Service Trends: General education teachers working with educational interpreters. *American Annals of the Deaf, 140*, 38-46.

Blanchfield, B., Feldman, J., & Dunbar, J. (2001). The severely to profoundly hearing-impaired population in the United States: Prevalence estimates and demographics. *Journal of the American Academy of Audiology, 12*, 183-189.

Bolster, L. A. (2005). *Time-compressed professionalization: The experience of public school Sign Language interpreters in mountain-plains states.* Unpublished doctoral dissertation, Virginia Polytechnic and State University, Blacksburg.

Bowe, F. (2003). Transition for deaf and hard of hearing students: A blueprint for change. *Journal of Deaf Studies and Deaf Education, 8*, 485-493.

Buklowski, W. M., Newcomb, A. F., & Hartup, W. W. (1996). *The company they keep: Friendships in childhood and adolescence.* Cambridge, UK: Cambridge University Press.

Cazden, C. (2001). *Classroom discourse: The language of teaching and learning.* Portsmouth, NH: Heineman.

Cokely, D. (1992). *Interpretation: A sociolinguistic model.* Burtonsville, MD: Linstok Press.

Connor, C. M., & Zwolan, T. A. (2004). Examining multiple sources of influence on the reading comprehension skills of children who use cochlear implants. *Journal of Speech, Language, and Hearing Research, 47*, 509-526.

Dean, R.K. & Pollard, R.Q. (2005). Consumers and service effectiveness in interpreting work: A practice profession perspective. In M. Marschark, R. Peterson & E. Winston (Eds.), *Sign language interpreting and interpreter education* (pp. 259 - 282). New York: Oxford University Press.

Foster, S. (1988). Life in the mainstream: Reflections of deaf college freshmen on their experiences in the mainstreamed high school. *Journal of Rehabilitation of the Deaf, 22*, 27-35.

Foster, S. (1989). Educational programs for deaf students: An insider perspective on policy and practice. In L. Barton (Ed.), *Integration: Myth or reality?* (pp. 57-82). London: The Falmer Press.

Frye, D., & Ziv, M. (2005). Teaching and learning as intentional activities. In B. D. Homer & C. S. Tamis-LeMonda (Eds.), *The development of social cognition and communication* (pp. 231-258). Mahwah, NJ: Lawrence Erlbaum.

Geers, A. (2003). Predictors of reading skill development in children with early cochlear implantation. *Ear & Hearing, 24*, 59S-68S.

Hartup, W. W. (1996a). Cooperation, close relationships, and cognitive development. In W. M. Buklowski, A. F. Newcomb & W. W. Hartup (Eds.), *The company they keep: Friendships in childhood and adolescence* (pp. 213 – 237). Cambridge, UK: Cambridge University Press.

Hartup, W. W. (1996b). The company they keep: Friendships and their developmental significance. *Child Development, 67*, 1–13.

Hertz-Lazarowitz, R. (1992). Understanding interactive behaviours: Looking at six mirrors if the classroom. In Hertz-Lazarowitz, R. & Miller, N. (Eds.). *Interaction in cooperative groups: The theoretical anatomy of group learning* (pp. 71-101). New York: Cambridge University Press.

Humphrey, J.A. & Alcorn, B.J. (1994). *So you want to be an interpreter? An introduction to Sign Language interpreting.* Amarillo, TX: H & H Publishers.

Janzen, T. & Shaffer, B. (in press). Intersubjectivity in interpreted interactions. In J. Zlatev, T. Racine, C. Sinha & E. Itkonen (Eds.), *The shared mind: Perspectives on intersubjectivity.* Philadelphia: John Benjamins.

Jones, B. (2004). Competencies of K-12 educational interpreters: What we need versus what we have. In E. Winston (Ed.), *Educational interpreting: How it can succeed.* (pp. 113-131). Washington, DC: Gallaudet University Press.

Jones, B. E., Clark, G. M., & Soltz, D. F. (1997). Characteristics and practices of Sign Language interpreters in inclusive education programs. *Exceptional Children, 63*, 257-268.

Kurz, K.B. (2004). *A comparison of deaf children's comprehension in direct communication and interpreted education.* Unpublished doctoral dissertation, University of Kansas, Lawrence.

Kurz, K. B., & Langer, E. C. (2004). Student perspectives on educational interpreting: Twenty deaf and hard of hearing students offer insights and suggestions. In E. A. Winston (Ed.), *Educational Interpreting: How it can succeed* (pp. 9 - 47). Washington, DC: Gallaudet University Press.

La Bue, M. A. (1998). *Interpreted education: A study of deaf students' access to the content and form of literacy instruction in a mainstreamed high school English class.* Unpublished dissertation, Harvard University, Cambridge.

Ladd, G. W. (1990). Having friends, keeping friends, making friends, and being liked by peers in the classroom: Predictors of children's early school adjustment? *Child Development, 61*, 1081-1100.

Lalonde, C.E. & Chandler, M.J. (1995). False belief understanding goes to school – on the social-emotional consequences of coming early or late to a first Theory of Mind. *Cognition and Emotion, 9*, 167-185.

Lang, H.G., Stinson, M.S., Kavanagh, F., Liu, Y., & Basile, M. (1998). Learning styles of deaf college students and teaching behaviours of their instructors. *Journal of Deaf Studies and Deaf Education, 4*, 16-27.

Langer, E.C. (2007). *Classroom discourse and interpreted education: What is conveyed to deaf elementary school students.* Unpublished Doctoral Dissertation, University of Colorado, Boulder.

Leekam, S. (1991). Jokes and lies: Children's understanding of intentional falsehood. In A. Whiten (Ed.), *Natural theories of mind* (pp. 159–174). Oxford, England: Blackwell.

Marschark, M. (2003). Cognitive functioning in deaf adults and children. In M. Marschark & P.E. Spencer (Eds.), *Oxford handbook of deaf studies, language, and education* (pp. 464 - 477). New York: Oxford University Press.

Marschark, M., Lang, H.G., & Albertini, J.A. (2002). *Educating deaf students: From research to practice.* New York, NY: Oxford University Press.

Marschark, M., Leigh, G., Sapere, P., Burnham, D., Convertino, C., Stinson, M., Knoors, H., Vervloed, M.P.J., Noble, W. (2006). Benefits of Sign Language interpreting and text alternatives for deaf student's classroom learning. *Journal of Deaf Studies and Deaf Education, 11*, 421-437.

Marschark, M., Sapere, P., Convertino, C., Seewagen, R. & Maltzan, H. (2004). Comprehension of Sign Language interpreting: Deciphering a complex task situation. *Sign Language Studies, 4*, 345-368.

Marschark, M., Sapere, P., Convertino, C., & Seewagen, R. (2005). Access to postsecondary education through Sign Language interpreting. *Journal of Deaf Studies and Deaf Education, 10*, 38-50.

Mertens, D.M. (1991). Teachers working with interpreters. *American Annals of the Deaf, 136*, 48-52.

Napier, J. (2004). Interpreting omissions: A new perspective. *Journal of Research and Practice in Interpreting, 6*, 117-142.

Newcomb, A. F., & Bagwell, C. (1996). The developmental significance of children's friendship relations. In W. M. Buklowski, A. F. Newcomb & W. W. Hartup (Eds.), *The company they keep: Friendship in childhood and adolescence*. Cambridge, UK: Cambridge University Press.

Padden, C., & Ramsey, C. (2000). American Sign Language and reading ability in deaf children. In C. Chamberlain, J. Morford & R. I. Mayberry (Eds.), *Language acquisition by eye* (pp. 165-189). Mahwah, NJ: Lawrence Erlbaum Associates.

Paul, P.V. (2003). Process and components of reading. In M. Marschark & P.E. Spencer (Eds.), *Oxford handbook of deaf studies, language, and education* (pp. 97 – 109). New York: Oxford University Press.

Peterson, C. (2004). Theory-of-mind development in oral deaf children with cochlear implants or conventional hearing aids. *Journal of Child Psychology & Psychiatry 45*, 1096-1106.

Piaget, J. (1928). *The child's conception of the world*. London: Routledge.

Portney, L.G. & Watkins, M.P. (2000). *Foundations of clinical research: Applications to practice*. Upper Saddle River, NJ: Prentice Hall Health.

Ramsey, C. L. (1997). *Deaf children in public schools: Placement, context, and consequences*. Washington, DC: Gallaudet University Press.

Richardson, J.. (in press). Approaches to studying among deaf students in higher education. In M. Marschark & P. Hauser (eds.), *Deaf cognition: Foundations and outcomes*. Oxford University Press.

Rogoff, B. (1990). *Apprenticeship in thinking*. Oxford, UK: Oxford University Press.

Roy, C. (2000). *Interpreting as a discourse process*. New York, Oxford University Press.

Ryan, A. M. (2000). Peer groups as a context for the socialization of adolescents' motivation, engagement, and achievement in school. *Educational Psychologist 35*, 101-111.

Scheibe, K., & Hoza, J. (1986). Throw it out the window! (The code of ethics? We don't use that here): Guidelines for educational interpreters. In M.L. McIntire (Ed.), *Interpreting: The art of cross-cultural medication: Proceedings of the Ninth National Convention of the Registry of Interpreters for the Deaf* (pp. 173-182). Silver Spring, MD: Registry of Interpreters for the Deaf.

Schick, B. (2004). Educational interpreting and cognitive development in children: Potential relationships. In E.A. Winston (d.), *Educational interpreting: How it can succeed* (pp. 73 – 87). Gallaudet Press, Washington, DC.

Schick, B. (2005). Final report: A national program for evaluating educational interpreters (Office of Special Education H325N010013).

Schick, B. (2007). EIPA Written Test. http://www.classroominterpreting.org/EIPA/standards/index.asp, retrieved July 17, 2007.

Schick, B. (in press). A model of learning in an interpreted education. In M. Marschark & P. Hauser (eds.), *Deaf cognition: Foundations and outcomes*. Oxford University Press.

Schick, B., de Villiers, P., de Villiers, J., & Hoffmeister, R. (2007). Language and theory of mind: A study of deal children. *Child Development, 78*, 376-396.

Schick, B., Williams, K. & L. Bolster (1999). Skill levels of educational interpreters. *Journal of Deaf Studies and Deaf Education 4*, 144-155.

Schick, B., Williams, K., & Kupermintz, H. (2006). Look who's being left behind: Educational interpreters and access to education for deaf and hard-of-hearing students. *Journal of Deaf Studies and Deaf Education 11*, 3-20.

Seal, B.C. (1998). Guidelines for inservicing teachers who teach with educational interpreters. *RID Views, 15,* 34-36.

Seal, B. (2000). Working with educational interpreters. *Language, Speech, & Hearing Services in the Schools, 31,* 15-25.

Seal, B. C. (2004). *Best practices in educational interpreting.* Boston, MA: Allyn & Bacon.

Seleskovitch, D. (1992). Fundamentals of the interpretive theory of translation. In J. Plant-Moeller (Ed.), *Expanding horizons (pp. 1 - 13).* Silver Spring, MD: Registry of Interpreters for the Deaf.

Setton, R. (1999). *Simultaneous interpreting: A cognitive-pragmatic analysis.* Philadelphia, PA: John Benjamins Publishing.

Sharan, S. (1990). Cooperative learning: A perspective on research and practice. In S. Sharan (Ed.), *Cooperative learning: Theory and research* (pp. 285 – 300). New York: Praeger Publishers.

Shaw, J.A., & Jamieson, J.R. (1997). Patterns of classroom discourse in an integrated elementary setting. *American Annals of the Deaf, 142,* 369-375.

Shroyer, E.H. & Compton, M.V. (1994). Educational interpreting and teacher preparation: An interdisciplinary approach. *American Annals of the Deaf, 139,* 472-479.

Sodian, B,, Zaitchik, D. & Carey, S. (1991). Young children's differentiation of hypothetical beliefs from evidence. *Children Development, 62,* 753-766.

Stedt, J.D. (1992). Issues of educational interpreting. In T. N. Kluwin, D. F. Moores & M. G. Gaustad (Eds.), *Toward effective public school programs for deaf students: Context, process, and outcomes* (pp. 83-99). New York: Teachers College, Columbia University.

Stewart, D. & Kluwin, T.N. (1996). The gap between guidelines, practice, and knowledge in interpreting services for deaf students. *Journal of Deaf Studies and Deaf Education, 1,* 29-39.

Stewart, D.A., Schein, J.D. & Cartwright, B.E. (2004). *Sign language interpreting: Exploring its art and science.* Boston, MA: Allyn & Bacon.

Traxler, C.B. (2000). The Stanford Achievement Test, 9th edition: National norming and performance standards for deaf and hard-of-hearing students. *Journal of Deaf Studies and Deaf Education, 5*, 337-348.

Turner, G.H. (2005). Toward real interpreting. In M. Marschark, R. Peterson & E. Winston (Eds.), *Sign language interpreting and interpreter education* (pp. 29 - 56). New York: Oxford University Press.

Wellman, H. M., & Lagattuta, K. H. (2004). Theory of mind for learning and teaching: The nature and role of explanation. *Cognitive Development, 19*, 479-497.

Winston, E. (2004). Interpretability and accessibility of mainstream classrooms. In E. Winston (Ed.), *Educational interpreting: How it can succeed* (pp. 132-167). Washington, DC: Gallaudet Press.

Witter-Merithew, A. & Dirst, R. (1982). Preparation and use of educational interpreters. In D.G. Sims, G.G. Walter, & R.L. Whitehead (Eds.), *Deaf and communication: Assessment training* (pp. 395-406). Baltimore: Williams & Wilkins.

Witter-Merithew, A., & Johnson, L. J. (2005). *Toward competent practice: Conversations with stakeholders*. Alexandria, VA: The Registry of Interpreters for the Deaf.

Yuill, N., & Perner, J. (1987). Exceptions to mutual trust: Children's use of second-order beliefs in responsibility attribution. *International Journal of Behavioral Development, 10*, 207–223.

Zawolkow, E.G. & DeFiore, S. (1986). Educational interpreting for elementary and secondary level hearing-impaired students. *American Annals of the Deaf, 131*, 26-28.

Summary of the conference discussion

Educator's ultimate goal is learning on the part of the student at a rate to match their peers. A clear understanding of the factors that affect learning in an interpreted education is essential to designing and evaluating services and outcomes. The more that is known about the factors that affect learning, the more multifaceted the approach to ensure accommodation can be.

There is tension between the interpreter's role of faithfully rendering as much of the classroom talk as they can (the interpretation part), and the aim of making sure the student understands as much as possible (the education part). The tension between who is responsible for ensuring learning (teacher, interpreter or both) is made more complex by the fact that there is a communication lag. As mentioned in the paper, Deaf learners receive the message slightly later than hearing students. This can make it more difficult for them to interrupt and ask questions, because the interpreter is always signing to keep up with everyone else's contributions; it takes a certain amount of confidence on the part of the deaf learner to 'interrupt' the interpreter and the class. This may mean that deaf learners have fewer opportunities to develop metacognitive skills of questioning, and assessing their own learning, and identifying what they do and do not understand - they are mostly on the 'receiving end' of communication, rather than being involved in a dynamic two way process. Yet from Vygotsky's perspective, it is students' interactions with others through language that most strongly influence their learning. Educational success or failure does not depend only on the individual ability of the learner - it also depends on the quality of the interaction between learners and teachers, and between groups of learners (Goodman et al 2002:12).

The paper included the term "illusion of inclusion". It seems that the presence of an interpreter allows the administrators to abdicate the responsibility for the deaf student's education and full inclusion. The acceptance of the profession and increased numbers of interpreters makes mainstreaming possible. Then the assumption is that the interpreter makes inclusion a reality, when in fact it only provides the possibility of full inclusion if so many other factors - involving student, parents, administrator, teacher, classroom environment and THEN the interpreter are addressed.

Though remedies are still needed at the level of the interpreter, this is a low level intervention. Real changes need to be made at the upper levels of educational planning. Many school administrators believe that mainstreaming "happens'" when deaf students and interpreters are present in their school. There is a great need to develop ways to show policy makers how much deaf children and children with cochlear implants are learning. Often hard-of-hearing children and children with CI's have functional speech and hearing skills in one-on-one conversations and naive professionals interpret this to mean that the student can do well in noisy classrooms, with multiple speakers, and competition for their visual attention. They "assess" in simple situations but the student has to survive in complex ones.

The presentation discussed social accessibility of the classroom. The nature of many classrooms is that teachers are relying on using dialogic processes and engaging students in a great deal of the co-construction of the learning event, and this is the place where interpreters struggle the most. When interpreters cannot represent the constructed discourse in the classroom in a way that makes sense in a visual-spatial language, this reinforces the "illusion" of an inclusive classroom.

The constructed discourse in the class is truly challenging for most interpreters to represent. This is an important question - how does this affect both learning as well as the d/hh student's entire sense of being a member of the community of minds in the classroom? Until we start really seeing the educational interpreter as a member of the "teaching team" in the classroom, this will be difficult to change. It would be beneficial if interpreters affect how these discussions are managed. For example, in most d/hh meetings, a light form of Robert's Rules of Order are followed, with the chair identifying speakers and pauses to allow eyes to move. The interpreter should be able to discuss with the teacher how to manage these discussions so they are more "interpretable". At present, that very rarely happens.

Currently, educational interpreters are not included in the decision making process and many classroom teachers and deaf educators are stuck in a model that is more appropriate for adult learners - come in, be a conduit, leave. Often the role of the interpreter is defined without reference to the educational context of the student and their educational needs. If a student needs an interpreter to assume a more active role to be able to learn - so be it. The focus should be on student learning. If educational interpreters need more training to accomplish this, we need to establish training models which achieve this. We also need to talk about this from the perspective of student learning.

In the future, cochlear implants will reduce the number of children in the profound range of deafness. CI's are not a cure, but moving a child from the profound to severe range is beneficial. When people talk about interpreting they mean this to be for a profoundly deaf child, but in the US much interpreting is done for students who have functional speech and auditory skills and more than half of educational interpreters report that they interpret for such children.

The presenter reported having conducted research on the development of ASL, manually coded English and oral communication, and many children do quite well with more English-based sign systems. There are advantages in using ASL as it is a natural Sign Language, but the research is not so clear cut. Many children have functional hearing skills which may make an English system a better choice.

Another issue which was discussed was the training educational interpreters receive. Interpreters in the legal arena have special training, interpreters in the medical arena have special training, interpreters in the arts have special training, why should educational interpreters not also have special training? Not only knowledge in subject areas so they understand vocabulary but courses in child development, language development, assessment, methods, child psychology, deaf education and special education. Then they would truly be a part of the educational team. This would truly benefit mainstreamed deaf children.

Goodman, S., Lillis, T., Maybin, J. and Mercer, N. (2002) Language and Literacy in a Changing World. Milton Keynes: The Open University

Giving Voice: Sign to Voice Interpreting for Hearing Consumers in K-12 settings in the United States, by Richard Brumberg

Introduction

You are an interpreter assigned full-time to an elementary school in a suburb of Chicago, Illinois. In one fourth-grade classroom, Student D, a bright Deaf-of-Deaf student is giving his report on the uses of electricity from an experiment he has done. At one point, he cites this example.[1]

Even if you don't know American Sign Language (ASL) - or any signed language - the visual presentation seems rich in language and in content. The facial expressions show a passion for the topic; the flow of the presentation indicates a well-thought-out report. As interpreters, we want to give a full interpretation coming from such a rich source.[2] Many interpreters find this to be a daunting task.

Interpreters have a general wariness towards voicing, let alone for students.[3] The age, language and cognitive levels of children and teenagers prove to be a worthy challenge for the voicing interpreter. On top of this, more and more Deaf and Hard of Hearing students from Deaf schools are transferring to public school settings. Just as these kids are becoming acclimated to a new environment, at least one hearing member, if not the whole school, is encountering Deaf culture and ASL for the first time. Compounding the matter further, there are outside components that have an unseen effect on the final interpretation: theories of interpreting, educational theories and governmental/ institutional policies, to name a few. All of these factors come together at each interpreting event almost

---

[1] Personal Interview. October, 2006. See VC4-1 in the Appendix.
[2] Note: For the purpose of this paper, the word *interpretation* and all of its forms means going from a signed language (ASL) to a spoken language (English).
[3] Tipton, 2006.

instantaneously. Given this, it is a wonder the interpreter ever ventures to open his/her mouth to give an interpretation! Yet, without a sufficient translation, the classroom teacher will not have access to a key component of student assessment - student's responses. More importantly, the Deaf student will not feel connected to his/her class and school if his/her voice is never heard.

How, then, can the interpreter give an accurate interpretation? How can we give Deaf students the "voice" everyone in the school so rightly deserves? This paper will address these questions using a three-pronged approach. In the first part, we will explore the theoretical backdrops to the interpreting event. Secondly, we will explore the stakeholders in the event, both in the foreground (present at the event) and in the background (not seen at the event). In the final section, we will focus on these elements to deliver more accurate interpretations. We will also take note of aspects unique to children and teen ASL production.

Behind the Scene: the Theories and Policies

As noted earlier, even before a sign is produced or a voice heard, there is a gamut of theories that surround the interpreting event. Consider the educational policies of the school. A country will most likely have an act, belief system or policy that is meant for all students and staff to comply with at any school. In a recent random search on the web, policies concerning curriculum, assessment and serving students with special needs were found in Great Britain, Australia, Japan, and the United States. In Australia and the US, the federal governments have given states/territories the responsibility of transforming the policies into detailed laws and actions. Because of this more individualised approach, states have organised their policies and labeled their terms differently.

In North Carolina, the Department of Public Instruction has specific rules for interpreting statewide testing, the End-of-Grade (EOG) Tests. These tests show student growth in the school year, specifically for reading, math and social studies. In the third, fifth, eighth and twelfth grade, these also serve as promotional tests -

which allow the student to move up to the next grade or graduate.[1] North Carolina allows for expository essays to be signed by the Deaf student, interpreted into English and then recorded on paper by a scripter. The essay is graded on features like how it is framed and the overall cohesiveness. New Jersey also follows this accommodation for "open-ended response(s)" on their tests (New Jersey Assessment of Skills and Knowledge [NJ ASK] and Grade Eight Proficiency Assessment [GEPA]). However, they include the rule that the student "must indicate all punctuation and must spell all key words".[2]

In another state, Illinois, has designed "Performance Descriptors" for each subject area. They further divide the descriptors into stages and, vis-à-vis the grade level, show a student's progression. (For instance, reaching Stage C for a third grader shows a higher progression than for a fourth grader.)[3]

These rubrics and accommodations speak volumes about the interpretation. For the first interpreting scenario, the English that the teacher hears about how to make a make-shift alarm will guide him/her to Student D's stage. For the interpreter who knows these rubrics, this is a double-edged sword. It may help the interpreter shape the voicing in a way that shows the student's stage. On the other hand, the interpreter may edit, "fill in" or raise the voicing to a higher level than what is shown. As mentioned before, this student seems confident of his analysis of the alarm but this does not necessarily prove the *validity* or the *totality* of his response. (I.e., I could say confidently, "2+7=5". The interpreter might not be sure if s/he heard "5" or "9" and might go with "9" because of my gusto.)

In another interpreting scene, suppose Student C, a hard of hearing girl in high school, is going to sign her essay about the differences between lunch at the hearing school and the Deaf school she

---

[1] North Carolina Public Schools. (2005). *Understanding the Individual Student Report: End-of-Grade Tests: Grades 3, 4 and 5*. Retrieved October 10, 2006.
http://www.ncpublicschools.org/docs/accountability/grade3_5parentteacherreportfinal.pdf.
[2] New Jersey Department of Education: Special Education. *Accommodations and Modifications of Test Administration Procedures for Statewide Assessments*. Retrieved October 10, 2006. http://www.nj.gov/njded/specialed/accom900.htm.
[3] For a more detailed explanation of this approach, visit
www.isbe.state.il.us/ils/science/pdf/descriptor_1-5.pdf. Illinois State Board of Education. (2002). Retrieved October 10, 2006.

attended. She signs the following.[1] In both North Carolina and New Jersey, the interpretation would be shaped to show her organisation: the first paragraph about the length and speed of the lunch line and the second paragraph about the payment method. Also, the English translation would indicate consistency in her comparison. This student maintains a clear contrastive grammar in her sign production: details about the hearing school always stay on her left and details about the Deaf school on her right. However, the interpreter in New Jersey would have to include any spelling of any words fingerspelled and would need to indicate any punctuation used.[2]

The other groups of ideas that affect the interpretation are educational and developmental theories. There is everything from behavioural modification to Whole Language to phonics to Piaget's Theory of Development. Though all of these are important for interpreters to know about, one theory that bears special relevance to our exploration is Vygotsky's Theory of Social Development. In short, his theory says that learning starts with social interaction and then is individualised. For instance, a baby moving his mouth muscles might form a smile by accident but when others start smiling and showing affection, the baby internalises the smile-making as meaningful. The theory also describes the Zone of Proximal Development as the social interaction which allows a student's level to develop higher than if he was alone.[3]

Consider this theory when we view the following student, Student A, a 14-year-old, describing how a graph is made and how you plot points.[4] You'll notice that A was prompted by the interviewer as his answers were fairly terse at the beginning. This is the type of engagement that teachers regularly employ when assessing how much a student has learned. The simple answer of "There's an x axis and y axis," would most likely trigger the teacher to ask what that

---

[1] See VC3-3.
[2] Indicating punctuation is a bit ambiguous. In all of the interviewers, the students showed clear visual markers of commas, periods, question marks and exclamation points. (Some by eye-gaze and blinking, others by hand-resting or body shifts.) Should the interpreter actually say "period" or would the intonation imply enough to the scripter to include the punctuation?
[3] *Social Development Theory*. 1994-2006. Retrieved October 9, 2006 from http://tip.psychology.org/vygotsky.html.
[4] See VC1-2.

means. Again, this prevents us from filling in more than what is said. The interaction allows the teacher to see how the student gives spontaneous answers and gives the student confidence to think on his own.

Setting the Stage: The Stakeholders[1]

Now that we've set the stage, the next step is to take note of who is present and who are the stakeholders - who has a vested interest in the voiced interpretation. We can divide the stakeholders into three groups: the speaker, the immediate audience and the secondary audiences.

The speaker in this case is the Deaf student. Ideally, we need to get as much information as we can prior to the interpretation. How long has the speaker been signing? Is the student from a Deaf family? Has she ever attended a school for the Deaf or a self-contained classroom? Even if he prefers ASL, he might code-switch to a more English-like sign system due to the audience and from reading what he has written.

Of equal importance is the student's age and personal make-up. One might ask such questions as:

- How old is the student? This can determine the vocabulary choice. ("Mom" versus "Mommy".)
- Is the student male or female? This, too, can determine how something is voiced.
- Is she educationally motivated or more socially oriented? (This might clue the interpreter in on how well the student can maintain the topic at hand.)
- Is he nervous about having an audience (or being on camera) or does he see this as an outlet to spread his wings?
- Does the student get easily frustrated when s/he's not understood or does s/he know how to deal with any misunderstanding? (This can help you with clarification techniques which are described later.)

---

[1] Roach, A. "Empowering the Young Deaf Community," *VIEWS* March 2002: 15.

- What are the student's favourite topics? (He'll try to bring that into any conversation he has.)
- How "fluid" is the student's use of the interpreter? Does she get the interpreter's attention first and sign TELL-HIM (less fluid) or does she simply start signing to the hearing listener (more fluid)?

All of these questions can apply to any Deaf speaker but because children can't always express these things directly, we will more than likely have to detect these qualities ourselves.

The hearing audience makes up the other half of those immediately present at the interpreting event. We should ask the above questions and include some others such as:

- Is the audience actively listening for answers like the scripter in North Carolina or s/he listening for entertainment?
- If the student is trying to lodge a complaint against another student during lunch, will the teacher be as interested if s/he's being interrupted from eating her meal?
- How knowledgeable is the immediate hearing audience about Sign Language, Deaf culture and the use of an interpreter?

Finally, we need to be cognisant of those who are not present but have a vested interest in the interpretation, such as:

- Deaf community stakeholders: the teacher of the Deaf, Deaf adults, parents of Deaf children, incoming Deaf students and interpreters.[1]
- Hearing community stakeholders: the grade level chair, the administration, parents of the hearing children, and the superintendent of the county and government officials.

Knowing all of the stakeholders will help us be more acutely aware of what we say in our interpretation.

---

[1] I am expanding on Amy Roach's list in her article, "Empowering the Young Deaf Community," *VIEWS* March 2002: 15.

On With the Show! Producing an Interpretation

We now come to the nitty gritty of our work and the missing piece for this event - the interpretation. Though there are a multitude of interpreting models, the Seleskovitch (1978), Gish (1996), Colonomos (1989, rev. 1997), and Cokely (1992) models are probably the most accepted and established of these. Seleskovitch's model provides the basic framework for interpreting between any two languages and the others build on that to focus on signed/spoken interpretation. Each one has a slightly variant shape but they all can be used to assist the interpreter with voicing. The Gish model focuses on the message; the Colonomos model deals with the message and what is happening in the interpreter's mind; the Cokely model takes a more sociolinguistic point of view.

One thing all these processes share is the part when the interpreter breaks down the form seen and gets to the meaning of the utterance. In order to get that full meaning, it would be helpful to wait until the "semantic intent" is "realised."[1] This is a critical piece as many interpreters, when stumped, go for a word-for-word voicing which bears little if any meaning. For example, in the earlier example of Student A describing how to use a graph, he signs: LOOK-FOR-ON-SIDE FOR *WORD* SAME-AS 4 COMMA 2 (*Italics mine*). "WORD" is the form but in the context of what was asked and by adding the "4 COMMA 4", we could voice this as, "You look for the *point* to graph. For example, it might be 4,2." As long as the teacher is looking for understanding the concept and not the surface label, this could be an appropriate interpretation.[2]

With this in mind, we are nearly ready to voice. Below are some strategies and situations unique to working with children and teens.

---

[1] Cokely. (June, 1992). A Sociolinguistic Model of the Interpreting Process: ASL & English. Linstock Press.
[2] Note: Just because this translation is a part of my presentation does not mean it's the only translation one can voice. My translations are merely a starting point for the reader to analyze and accept, or reject and change completely.

Voice Over Voice

As mentioned in the previous section, we need to know the educational background of the speaker. There are a number Deaf and hard-of-hearing students who have received cochlear implants and are taught to speak for themselves first when dealing with a hearing person. Others may switch to voicing because they are bilingual. Still others will try to use their voice because they don't want the interpreter, a grown-up, hanging around them every minute of the school day. A good rule of thumb for the interpreter would be to remain in the area in case there is a misunderstanding. Most of the time, one of the two consumers will come up and ask you to interpret what is not understood. Just remember that one of your main responsibilities is to "[r]ender the message faithfully by conveying the content and spirit of what is being communicated, using language most readily understood by consumers..."- in this case, Spoken English.[1]

On the other side of the spectrum, there is the Deaf voice which may or may not be related to what is signed. When it is related, it tends to mark emphasis of what is being signed. For example, when talking about the recent events at Gallaudet University, Student D's voice keeps popping up during verbal and physical protests.[2] This would indicate the immensity of the situation. An equivalent interpretation might warrant one's inflection to stress words that mean the same thing, as in: "So *tons* of people started marching and *every* driver that came by would *blast* their horns and stick their thumbs out to tell the marchers to keep going." By adding this dimension to the interpretation, we are also supporting the idea that the Deaf voice can be a linguistic entity and not just random sounds.

Grammatically Correct: Another Point of View

In many interpreting workshops about voicing, we are told that we need to expand our English vocabulary. However, many of us take that to mean just to learn words at a higher register. What would

---

[1] Registry of Interpreters for the Deaf. (2005). NAD-RID Code of Professional Conduct. Retrieved September, 2006 from http://rid.org/codeofethics.pdf
[2] VC4-6.

happen if we used too high a register when the student was speaking in front of her peers? The other kids might view her as a know-it-all or may think that the interpreter is explaining what to do! As an example, suppose a boy from Student C's math class was absent yesterday and asks her what does a box-and-whiskers graph mean. She responds thusly…[1]

If we were to voice this in perfect English and use big terminology like "The zeros are positioned at the origin of the number line and the numbers increase incrementally by ones to the right…", the hearing student might walk away more confused than when he started. I would advise using more conversational lingo and using a less formal register. One interpretation might be "You've got the number line and the zero's right in the middle. Then the positive numbers keep goin' up to the right…" "Got" and "goin' " are not grammatically correct for formal English but they are perfectly acceptable for kids when they're talking together.

One way to handle this is if you have any prep time, you might ask another teacher in the same grade if you can observe his/her class. Listen to how the kids talk - particularly the difference between when they're talking to adults and when they're talking to each other. You'll find a whole lexicon of words you'll be able to use to make the Deaf student feel more a part of the crowd.

Use of Space

With young children and teens, sign production is not restricted to a compact, centralised area of space. They can be very creative in their use of space, as in Student D's explanation of a chemistry experiment or Student E's description of an American football game.[2] By the same token, like their hearing counterparts, Deaf kids can mumble or speak too loudly. A way for the interpreter to combat this is to keep his eyes right at the area between the chin and upper chest. The interpreter will be able to catch if anything is being signed peripherally. Following this area is much more effective than trying to follow the hands.

---

[1] VC3-4.
[2] VC4-3.

Isn't There a Sign/Word for That? ASL/English Expansions

ASL expansions are "the amplification of certain concepts of English in order to create meaning and be linguistically appropriate in ASL."[1] First proposed by Lawrence in 1994, these techniques have helped non-native signers to become more native-like. Building on this, Kelly (2004) and Finton and Smith have suggested using compression techniques which would "create meaning and maintain linguistic appropriateness" when voicing.[2] One kind of expansion is explaining by example. In this technique, examples are strung together to form an equivalent meaning in ASL. In the earlier sample, Student B said that he loved computers, in particular Dell Technologies. When asked if he knows what his job entails, he says, YES, YOU-KNOW PRACTICE CREATIVE^{++} (2h, alt.) DRAW, MEASURE WEIRD GAME COOL WELL-THAT TECHNOLOGY.[3] All of the verbs signed indicate the idea of designing games. This could be voiced as "At work, I'll get to make extreme video games!"

By the same token, some words in ASL need to be expanded because they tap into culturally rich realities, an idea described by Cokely (2001). For instance, suppose a hearing teacher with no knowledge of Deaf culture listened to Student D's retelling of the events at Gallaudet. Just voicing "hearing" and "deaf" for HEARING and DEAF would not convey the deeper meaning- particularly when culture is at the heart of this story. One idea might be to expand the first time these signs are used. For instance, "There was one hearing man who wasn't like the Deaf students and wanted the job and there two Deaf men who *were* like the Deaf students." Our hope is that it would show HEARING and DEAF as cultural identity markers. Remember, though, that the English should match the age of the student. This makes the expansion more challenging since the signer is of a younger age.

---

[1] National Technical Institute for the Deaf. (2004) *NTID Papers and Publications 2004*. Retrieved October 5, 2006 from
http://www.rit.edu/~493www/etrr/pages/PandP2004/teaandinter.htm
[2] Finton, L and Smith, R. (2005). Compression Strategies: ASL to English Interpreting. *Journal of Interpretation,* 49.
[3] VC2-2.

Conclusion

We now have a better idea of what lies before us when we interpret in school settings. However, this paper just scratches the surface of the challenges and strategies of interpreting from ASL to English when working with children and teens. Due to the experience of the author, we were limited to specific examples in the United States. It is hoped that this paper will be a springboard for discussion of strategies and issues for professionals world-wide who work in educational settings with Deaf students.

References

Cokely, D. (June, 1992). A Sociolinguistic Model of the Interpreting Process: ASL & English. Linstock Press.

Cokely, D. (2001). Interpreting Culturally Rich Realities:Research Implications for Successful Interpretations. *Journal of Interpretation*.

Colonomos, B. M. (1989). *The interpreting process: A working model.* Manuscript.

Finton, L and Smith, R. (2005). Compression Strategies: ASL to English Interpreting. *Journal of Interpretation*

Gish, S. (1996) *The interpreting process: Introduction and skills practice, the Gish approach to information processing.*

Illinois State Board of Education. (2002). Retrieved October 10, 2006 from www.isbe.state.il.us/ils/science/pdf/descriptor_1-5.pdf..

Kelly, J. (2004). *ASL-to-English Interpretation: Say it Like They Mean it.* Dubuque, Iowa: Kendall/Hunt.

National Technical Institute for the Deaf. (2004) *NTID Papers and Publications 2004.* Retrieved October 5, 2006 from http://www.rit.edu/~493www/etrr/pages/PandP2004/teaandinter.htm

New Jersey Department of Education: Special Education. *Accommodations and Modifications of Test Administration Procedures for Statewide*

Assessments. Retrieved October 10, 2006 from http://www.nj.gov/njded/specialed/accom900.htm.

North Carolina Public Schools. (2005). *Understanding the Individual Student Report: End-of-Grade Tests…* Retrieved October 10, 2006 from
http://www.ncpublicschools.org/docs/accountability/grade3_5parentteacherreportfinal.pdf.

Registry of Interpreters for the Deaf. (2005). NAD-RID Code of Professional Conduct. Retrieved September, 2006 from http://rid.org/codeofethics.pdf

Roach, A. (2002, March)."Empowering the Young Deaf Community," *VIEWS.*

Seleskovitch, D. (1978). *Interpreting for international conferences.* Washington DC: Pen and Booth.

Social Development Theory. 1994-2006. Retrieved October 9, 2006 from http://tip.psychology.org/vygotsky.html.

Tipton, C. (2006, February) "Unique Challenges of Interpreting from ASL to English," *VIEWS.*

Appendix - Transcriptions of Selected Video Captures

Note: Where possible, I have purposefully glossed signs with words that would not appear in the final translation. This is to prevent the reader from thinking that my words are the final say. The glosses are merely a starting point for the paper and further discussion. Words that are in superscript and in quotes show English on the mouth without any corresponding sign. Words in lower-case in parentheses indicate body movements/descriptions. Any interviewer's questions/statements are in italicised English.

For those who do not use ASL and are interested in a possible translation for any of these transcriptions, please feel free to contact the author at raslterp@yahoo.com. (Again, this is a "possible" translation to allow others to come up with other versions of a translation.)

Guide to the glosses:

X= sign
X^{++} = repeated sign
X!= signed emphatically
X? (rhet.)= rhetorical question
C+A+T= word is spelled out
#ALL= lexicalised fingerspelled word
2h= made with both hands
2h, alt.= made with both hands in alternating fashion
X+Y= compound
$CL_{A(...)}$= classifier$_{handshape\ (description)}$
$CL_{A\ mod.}$= modified handshape "X"

Student A

VC1-2

What's something you've learned in math?

SAME-AS Y A+X+I+S AND SECOND-ON-LIST X A+X+I+S. Y A+X+I+S ITSELF BAR-GO-UP-AND-DOWN IS NEGATIVE AND POSITIVE. X A+X+I+S BAR-GO-LEFT-AND-RIGHT NEGATIVE-ON-LEFT, POSITIVE-ON-RIGHT.

How do you use the graph?

LOOK-FOR-ON-SIDE FOR WORD SAME-AS 4 COMMA 2. LOOK-FOR-ON-GRAPH 4, DOT-ON-HORIZONTAL; DOT-ON-VERTICAL 2. POINTS-MEET-AT-INTERSECTION-ON-GRAPH MAKE-DOT.

Student B

VC2-2

What are your favorite subjects?

#OH UMM... MATH, SECOND-ON-LIST, COMPUTER. YES, FASCINATE D+E+L+L TECHNOLOGY. DESIGN+PERSON.

What kind of job did you say you wanted?

DESIGN DON'T-KNOW THAT I IDIOT THERE-YOU-GO DESIGN-PERSON. MAKE VOCABULARY GAME, VIDEO-GAME, INTERESTED GAME MAKE WEIRD GAME D+E+L+L, INCREASE MY CREATE^{++} (2h, alt.) THAT.

YES, YOU-KNOW PRACTICE CREATIVE^{++} (2h, alt.) DRAW, MEASURE WEIRD GAME COOL WELL-THAT TECHNOLOGY.

Student C

VC3-3

Is lunchtime at the school for the Deaf different from when you attended the hearing school?

HEARING SCHOOL THEIR $_{(to\ left)}$ LUNCH DIFFERENT THAN DEAF-SCHOOL LITTLE-BIT DIFFERENT.

Was there a long line at the public school?

YES. LINE-OF-PEOPLE.

And at the Deaf school?

(to right) LITTLE-BIT NOT MUCH LONG-LINE TO "the" END "of the" HALL BUT (move left) POINT-TO-LEFT HEARING SCHOOL HALL LONG-LINE! (move right) DEAF MAYBE SHORT LINE LINE-MOVE-ALONG PERSON-MOVE-UP SHORT AND (move left) AND HEARING SCHOOL HAVE MUST HAVE CARD-HANG-IN-FRONT CARD SWIPE-THROUGH. (move right) DEAF-SCHOOL NONE GO-ON-THROUGH BUT WITH-THE-UNDERSTANDING MAKE SURE KNOW YOU. IF NEW MAKE SURE WRITE YOU MAKE SURE KNOW IDENTITY YOU-ALL. IF NEW MAKE SURE HOLD-BACK FILL-OUT-PAPER[++] THEN FREE LUNCH. BUT (shift left) DEPENDS ON MY IF MY PARENTS WORK[++], (nod head) HAVE-TO TREAT FOR HEARING SCHOOL LUNCH. BUT(shift right) HERE FREE. LUNCH FREE LUNCH.

VC3-4

What is a box- and-whiskers graph?

BOX WHISKER[++] NAME OF…SAME-AS..LET'S-SEE…
LINE NUMBER LINE ZERO-AT-CENTER (2h) ONE, TWO, THREE (to the right) , NEGATIVE ONE, NEGATIVE TWO, NEGATIVE THREE (to the left) . THEN TELL-YOU WHICH I+S MOST NUMBER #OR GREAT NUMBER THEN "put" DOT-ON-PAPER-ACROSS-IN-LINE. THEN WHEN FINISH THAT DRAW-BOX THEN MAKE LINE SEE BIG AND LESS-THAN-NUMBER. LINE LINE-GO-DIAONALLY-UP-TO-RIGHT, LINE-GO-DIAGONALLY-UP-TO-LEFT. WHISKER BOX WHISKER LINE-GO-OUT. "That's" WHY CALLED THAT I THINK.

Student D

VC4-1

What did you learn about batteries?

IF BATTERY HAVE BLACK HOW IF STEAL+PERSON SOMETIMES IN YOUR HOUSE HUH? NOT-KNOW ME SAME-AS-YOU NOTHING. HOW LIGHT-FLASH^{++} ALARM? KNOW HOW (rhet.)? I USE MY TEACHER SCIENCE TEACHER'S CL$_1$ (shape of rectangle) WITH D C+E+L+L BATTERY PUT-ON-BOARD ATTACH-TO STAYS-BY-ITSELF. TWO W+I+R+E+S WIRE-COME-OUT-AT-TWO-ENDS WITH LIGHT WIRES-MEET-AT-SAME-POINT. PAPER WEDGE-BETWEEN WILL LIGHT-GO-OUT WITH TAPE ON PAPER. KNOW DOOR PUT-PAPER-ON TAPE-TO STAYS-THERE. DOOR HIDE-BEHIND QUIET. ARRIVE SHUSH STEAL+PERSON PROWL-TO-UP OPEN-DOOR-WIDE. ITSELF COME-OUT, PAPER RELEASE-FROM-CATCH LIGHT-GOES-ON-INSTANTANEOUSLY! (nod yes) PAPER-COME-OUT KNOW CAUGHT-IN-THE-ACT ARREST!

VC4-3

What other experiments have you done?

CHEMISTRY HARD! PATIENT POUR CHEMICAL. YES BEFORE ME RABBIT I TRY RABBIT FAKE RABBIT (pose as rabbit). TRY PINK FILL-UP POUR-ON APPENDAGE-POP-OUT-ON-EACH-SIDE ARM BECOME LEG BECOME WING^{++}. POUR BLUE UP-NECK, WHOLE-NECK COME-OFF BECOME BIRD FACE HEAD BODY. POUR GREEN FAST-BECOME BODY PERFECT BODY BIRD BODY
DOWN-TO-LEGS POUR-CHEMICAL^{++} (2h, alt.) BECOME BIRD WINGS-EXTENDED.

VC4-6

Do you know what's been going on at Gallaudet University?

(nod yes) ONE WOMAN HEARING WANT CAN MAN RUN-TO LEARN SIGN LANGUAGE LEARN^{++}. SAY LIST-OF-THREE. PICK-THUMB^{++}, HEARING MAN. PICK-POINTER, PICK-MIDDLE-FINGER, TWO-ON-POINTER-AND-MIDDLE^{++} DEAF MAN. HEARING WOMAN POINT-AT-THUMB! WAVE-NO!

(2h) NO++ (2h) PLEASE (shake head) HEARING MAN DEAF MAN++ BEG-PLEASE. (shake head) NO,NO. MESS. FINE! PARADE!++ WRONG. #CAR VEHICLE-COME-FROM-EACH-DIRECTION, PUT-THUMB-UP BLOW-HORN CL_B (vehicle moving by in either direction) . WOMAN LOOK-AT-ALL DON'T-WANT. WITHDRAW! TURN-DOWN! STUNNED ACCEPT. PRESIDENT PUT-UP-WITH.

Who's the president now?

NOW? HEARING.

Summary of the conference discussion

A delegate who is a teacher had noticed that many students may be unclear, sloppy or off-the-point when signing in class. This may be due to them being poor communicators generally. Sometimes interpreters try to "make sense" of what a student is saying if they are unclear and therefore mask more serious language/communication issues. In Interpreter Training Programmes (ITPs) most of the emphasis is placed on expressive sign skills and not voicing skills and therefore many interpreters in the mainstream often blame themselves for not understanding the student. Also, simply understanding what is signed is different to being able to take in what is being signed and interpreting it into spoken English simultaneously. As interpreters gain receptive experience, they can more readily recognise when the message is unclear or off the point as opposed to valid and well-constructed messages that they simply cannot interpret because of weak voicing skills. Usually interpreter training programmes prepare interpreters to work with deaf adults, and therefore they are unprepared for the differences with working with deaf children.

Many interpreters' directional preference is for voice to sign interpreting. For interpreters whose first language is a spoken one, the opposite should be true. Interpreting into one's first language should be the preferred mode, since, in our second language, our receptive skills are stronger than our expressive skills. Additionally, when interpreting into one's second language (where bilingualism has not been achieved), one doesn't have the skills in the target language to monitor one's work with maximum acuity. Thus, we may think we're rendering a good interpretation when we may not be. To compound this problem, Deaf people are accustomed to "re-interpreting" in their minds an interpreted message in order to understand it, so there is often no indication that the interpretation may be flawed. Most interpreters get more experience interpreting from a spoken to a signed language, so the comfort with interpreting in this direction is no surprise.

Some positive things which can help interpreters to voice better are:

- Working in a team of interpreters, so that the student's signing style can be analysed collectively and this can help the individual interpreters comprehend and voice more accurately.

- Working with the same students everyday helps an interpreter to monitor language and to get comfortable with his/her signing.

- Hanging out with other hearing students helps to figure out what the lingo and the attitude of the students is.

- Working with deaf adults to get more practice. Sometimes educational interpreters can get comfortable in their positions and their skills stagnate. Working with Deaf adults not only helps with signing/receptive skills, but it serves as a reminder that the kids we work with now are the future of the Deaf community.

- Watching and listening to the movies, music, games and reading the popular books for the age group who are being interpreted to learn more vocabulary.

- Establishing good practices in the classroom, for example, is if the teacher asks a question, no one can answer the question until after it has been interpreted. Similarly, the interpreter should voice the Deaf student's response even after everyone else has responded, so that the Deaf student has the chance to contribute equally.

- Increasing lag-time to wait for "semantic intent", even if this creates pauses in the communication.

At the conference there was a long discussion about the need to voice for children in an appropriate manner, by using slang or voicing very informally when their presentation is 'slouchy'. After all, hearing children mumble, slouch, etc. too. It can be difficult to include the "slouchiness" of children's sign production. It would seem counter-productive to mumble just like the student did, as this can hinder communication, however, it is still an aspect interpreters should convey. In many countries the interpreter's code of ethics or professional conduct states that interpreters should render the message faithfully by conveying the content and spirit of what is being communicated. In the case of voicing for children, mumbling and slouching are part of the spirit of the speaker. So by mumbling slightly during voicing, the hearing listener has the chance to ask for clarification, as they would do with a hearing child. When working in schools it is useful to give teachers a heads-up about what the sign production should look like prior to classroom presentation. A lot of times, teachers grade on clarity and volume but they don't know what that looks like in a signed language. Some initial guidance can help them remember these elements once they start grading.

In terms of voicing for children, it is important that the interpreter is comfortable with the style or register of the child. Deaf children are often not clear or use 'intimate register' - name signs or references that only those close to them will know. Only when the interpreter understands how the child is using language can s/he render an effective equivalent in a spoken language. This requires spending time in the domain of the Deaf child. Merely being in the school setting is insufficient since (in a mainstream setting anyway) the child is often more of a passive participant. The interpreter shouldn't try to "sound" like a child (just as a female interpreter doesn't try to sound male when voicing for a Deaf man). Instead, it is better to use turns-of-phrase and tone qualities that hearing children who possessed the same social or emotional traits of the Deaf children.

If Sign Language and English are the student's second and third language and they are not fluent in the language that the class is being conducted in or unable to articulate their point, or comment clearly, then is it the interpreter's responsibility to use their knowledge of the subject matter to fill in the blanks or make sense of the student's comments? Many interpreter's feel it is their responsibility to fix the message and if they do not they are regarded as an unskilled interpreter. Many students in graduate studies at major universities are from foreign countries and they are still trying to acquire the skill of articulating their thoughts and ideas in English. When the hearing students have trouble making their point clearly, the other students will ask for clarification. If interpreters fix the message or comment from the deaf student, then the interpreter may be robbing them of the ability to grow and learn from their mistakes.

The work of Robyn Dean and Robert Pollard found that the listener is taking in information from the interpretation - not the source. This may sound obvious, but the listener is assuming that's what the speaker said. For instance, suppose a Deaf student is reading about volcanoes. The sentence reads, "Smoke comes out of the opening." The student signs, SMOKE-CIGARETTE COME OUT #OF #THE OPEN-DOOR. If the interpreter just voices the printed sentence, they are masking the student's comprehension and the teacher will conclude that the student understands. And the student won't know she's signing non-conceptually. It is worth the interpreter looking for an approach within the interpretation before using narration. In this case, the interpreter might voice "Smoke cigarette come outside of the open the door." It sounds bizarre... and that is what the teacher should be looking for. It would be just like a hearing kid saying "Smoke comes out off the opening." In this way, the teacher will experience the "misreading" of the text.

What can be challenging for an interpreter is not when they cannot understand the source message, but if the source message is nonsense. If what the student is saying doesn't make sense it should be conveyed, but how does the interpreter voice "equivalent" nonsense? Especially if the student's needs will be addressed, if the interpreter simply glosses the signs out loud, it is hard to add affect. So punctuation might be correct, articulation may be good, but it's a jumble of concepts. When that happens it is tempting for the interpreter to just make sense of it, skip it, or wait until it connects with something and make future sense of it.

Some strategies may be to change pitch/intonation at weird times or add narration outside of the interpretation, by saying, for example, "The student is signing all over the place and is not forming any full sentences."

One delegate was called upon in the past to interpret Jabberwocky. Unless the rendition is as nonsensical as the original then it is not accurately translated. Interpreters we are looking for meaning. If someone isn't making sense perhaps the best interpretation is the one that says so.

It is a hard judgment call for an interpreter as to what to do when faced with interpreting a signed message that isn't making sense. Firstly they have to decide whether they are not understanding because of their own lack of skill, or does the message truly not make sense? Second, if the message isn't making sense, how can it be expressed clearly in English so the hearing party/parties are getting the 'real' message? Thirdly, if the interpreter chooses to add narration, they have to try to figure out how to convert what's visually 'wrong' into an auditory explanation that will allow the hearing audience to draw a conclusion about the cause of the disfluent message. Most interpreters are not equipped to evaluate the signing of their students, let alone those that are particularly idiosyncratic. To say that it is "nonsense" may be misleading. The key is where the communication breakdown is, at the morphological and phonological level, not just semantic. Sometimes there is a "sense" to their "nonsense".

Another issue is that many students use a signing system, rather than Sign Language, and do not use conceptually accurate signing. For example, a student using Signed Exact English will sign every suffix (-ing, -ness, etc.), or may only use one sign for the word "run". For the interpreter, it can be difficult to make English sentences when having to concentrate on a lexical/morphological level before they can weed out the point of the message.

The presentation stated that North Carolina public schools "allows for expository essays to be singed by the Deaf student, interpreted into English and then recorded on paper by a scripter". How can a students performance be fairly and accurately measured when their responses are so dependent upon the knowledge, skill and the interpreter's perception of the student's stage?

In Scotland, deaf candidates may elect to sign examination responses to camera for their national examinations (excluding English). The responses are then translated into English (usually by teachers of the deaf but occasionally interpreters). One of the stipulations of the awarding body is that the translator be familiar with the signing candidate. The submitted translations are later checked by a deaf review team appointed by the SQA (Scottish Qualifications Authority) for accuracy. The advantage of course, is having time to translate the student's response via the recorded image which can be rewound as required to make the most accurate translation - essential in such important examinations.

Another delegate described the practice in her area in the US, stating that a scribe sits in front of a computer with the student sitting to the side. Both are vidoetaped while the student signs their answers in ASL to the scribe who translates the answers into an English equivalent. When the answer is complete, the scribe and student switch seats and the student may make any adjustments/corrections/changes they wish. The tapes are kept on file in case there is a question of the scribe rendering too much "help'" during the test.

The allowance for essays to be signed, interpreted and then scripted is a good idea. It does, however, put the deaf student at a disadvantage. The non-deaf student has the advantage of being able to write, read and re-read, erase, re-order events, etc. when writing an essay. To give the deaf student a level playing field, is s/he given extra time to map out the essay before presenting it in sign? There are also few model essays in signed languages, whereas there is a plethora of revision material in written form.

There can be situations when the interpreter struggles to voice in a natural way and this can lead to the student being disadvantaged. For example, during a presentation, the Deaf student may provide preparation material by giving the interpreter a copy of his or her presentation, completely scripted. This can lead to the voice-over sounding unnatural. Preparation is the key in providing a good voice-over in this situation. Not only getting a copy of their written report but asking the student to show the interpreter their presentation at least once and talking about the information is key. It is important that the student knows that if they have not prepped their interpreter they are not ready. If the interpreter doesn't know the vocabulary they want or need the interpreter to use, then their work will have been for nothing. Also, in a situation where the student is already going to be nervous, preparation will minimise the need for interruptions.

Language and Learning by Deaf Students by Loes Wauters, Marc Marschark, Patricia Sapere and Carol Convertino

A more extensive version of this paper, by Marschark and Wauters appeared in Marschark, M. & Hauser, P.C., Editors (2008). Deaf cognition: Foundations and outcomes. New York: Oxford University Press.

Do deaf students learn in the same ways that hearing students learn? If communication barriers in the mainstream classroom are removed, do they learn as much and as quickly as their age-mates? Alternatively, is there a benefit to an academic setting with a trained teacher of the deaf? Such questions involve aspects of language and cognition as well as pedagogy and academic curriculum issues. The fact that we do not yet have definitive answers to any of them also indicates that these questions are not simple. Here, we suggest the possibility that interactions between language comprehension and cognition underlie differences and challenges observed in learning by deaf students at a more basic level than has been considered previously. Indeed, when the existing literature is viewed from this perspective, it appears far less contradictory and more informative than is typically assumed.

Evidence to be described below suggests that deaf and hearing students have somewhat different knowledge, that the organisation of that knowledge is measurably different in the two populations, and that they employ different cognitive strategies in learning and memory tasks. Such variability makes educational research involving deaf learners far more complex than might be assumed (Marschark, Convertino, & LaRock, 2006). Issues associated with the debate over integrated versus separate schooling of deaf children are particularly relevant here. However, it is rare that investigators consider the role of either psychological factors or language skills in academic achievement. Some investigators have sought to identify the characteristics of optimal academic environments for deaf learners, but most of these have involved surveys of perceptions rather than direct empirical assessment (e.g., Lang, Dowaliby, & Anderson, 1994; Lang, McKee, & Conner, 1993; Long & Beil, 2005), and thus we cannot yet be sure what kinds of educational interventions would be optimal for deaf students.

Even with such important questions remaining, the difference in outcomes when teachers know how deaf students think and learn is now clear. Several studies have demonstrated that deaf students tend to learn significantly less in mainstream college classrooms than their hearing peers, despite having highly-skilled interpreters and instructors who utilise appropriate classroom techniques for teaching deaf students (e.g., collaboration with interpreters, providing notes) (Jacobs, 1977; Marschark, Sapere, Convertino, Seewagen, & Maltzen, 2004; Marschark, Sapere, Convertino, & Seewagen, 2005; Marschark, Pelz, et al., 2005, Marschark, Leigh, et al., 2006). Marschark, Sapere, et al. (2008) conducted a series of experiments that yielded a somewhat different result. What was different in that study compared to the earlier investigations was that each of the teachers in their four experiments had considerable experience and skill in teaching deaf students; all had won awards for excellence in teaching (deaf students).

Independent of whether teachers were deaf or hearing, signed for themselves or used an interpreter, used simultaneous communication (speech and sign together) or voice-off ASL, the deaf students gained just as much as hearing students, despite the fact that pretests showed them to start at a significant disadvantage in content knowledge. We assume that if such teachers were available to deaf students in mainstream primary and secondary classrooms, that disadvantage might never have developed in the first place – but the hypothesis remains to be tested. Further, it is going to take a considerable amount of work to determine precisely what teachers who are familiar with deaf students do differently than those who are not and then develop ways to impart that information efficiently and economically to teachers in mainstream classrooms (Antia, 2007). The heterogeneity of today's population of deaf students is going to make this a complex task, and one that is going to require collaboration between researchers and practitioners across a variety of contexts. Such work holds great promise however.

Learning and learning how to learn begin in the home. The vast majority of hearing parents, however, are unfamiliar with the implications of hearing loss, the viability of Sign Language as a first language, and the difficulty encountered by deaf children in acquiring spoken language. It therefore should not be surprising that most of them eagerly embrace the recommendations of the early EHDI (early hearing detection and intervention) professionals for "speech first." There has never been any evidence that early Sign Language interferes with the acquisition of spoken language and, in fact, there is now considerable evidence that deaf children's spoken language abilities are either independent of or supported by early use of Sign Language in the home (e.g., Moeller, 2000; Yoshinaga-Itano, 2003).

Yet the recent pragmatic emphasis on spoken language for deaf children, accompanying the increasing popularity of cochlear implants, has not been accompanied by research concerning the acquisition of receptive versus production skills in real-world settings like the classroom. What evidence is available for children without implants suggests that spoken language is not the panacea that many parents are led to believe (Arnold, Palmer, & Lloyd, 1999; Lloyd, Lieven, & Arnold, 2005).

Several studies have compared learning via Sign Language interpreting versus simultaneous communication from an instructor (e.g., Cokely, 1990; Leigh & Power, 1998; Marschark, Sapere, et al., 2008). Other studies of classroom learning by deaf students have compared the effectiveness of transliteration (English-based signing) and interpretation (in ASL) in the classroom, usually at the college level (e.g., Livingston, Singer, & Abramson, 1994; Murphy & Fleischer, 1977). Such studies have not demonstrated an advantage for any particular mode of signing by instructors (Marschark, Sapere, et al., 2008) or by interpreters (Marschark, Sapere, et al., 2004; Marschark, Sapere, et al., 2005), indicating that deaf students have sufficiently flexible language skills to be able to utilise diverse modes of signed communication, at least by college age. Although these studies have indicated that deaf college students, on average, come away with less information from interpreted classes than do their hearing peers, results have indicated that not to be a consequence of either interpreting quality or student language/communication skills. Recent research suggests that students' academic preparation, prior content knowledge, and teachers' abilities to match their teaching methods to deaf students' learning styles and knowledge are far more potent predictors of learning than those communication variables or demographic factors (e.g., parental hearing status, hearing thresholds, modality of communication), but more research is clearly needed.

There also have been several studies that have compared classroom learning by deaf students who use spoken language versus Sign Language. Those studies typically have utilised spoken lectures supported by Sign Language interpreting, so students with both orientations are provided with both speech and sign. Experiments have manipulated the nature of the signed message (e.g., two-dimensional or three-dimensional, simultaneous communication or sign only), the physical relationship of an instructor's lecture to visual materials (angular separation), and the complexity of signs produced in the periphery. While Pelz et al. describe the results of the eye tracking part of these investigations, we have never observed significant differences in learning between the signing and oral students (e.g., Marschark, Pelz, et al. 2005; Marschark, Sapere, et al., 2008) despite a variety of studies suggesting that skilled deaf signers have greater acuity for peripheral visual stimuli (Dye et al., 2008). Marschark, Pelz, et al. (2005) therefore concluded that the enhanced visuospatial acuity that apparently accrues to signers in terms of sensitivity to stimulus change in the periphery may have little effect on functioning "in the real world."

The kinds of findings we have described clearly contradict many of the strong statements encountered about the advantages of one communication mode or the other. At the same time, they suggest that there may be other studies that have failed to find differences between spoken language and Sign Language in various contexts, but their null findings remain unpublished. Unfortunately, without reports of such null results, anecdote and assumption continue to be taken as fact and influence parental decisions about educational placement for their deaf children.

A similar situation arises when one considers deaf students' reading. It appears that word identification is a necessary skill underlying text comprehension, one that interacts with other linguistic and cognitive skills (Bebko & Metcalf-Haggert, 1997). Similar arguments could be mounted with regard to word identification in the comprehension of spoken language and for sign identification in the comprehension of Sign Language, but relevant studies have not yet been undertaken. The issue of sign identification might be particularly important in the larger context of language comprehension and learning. Even if young deaf children (e.g., of deaf parents) have early vocabularies comparable in size to those of their hearing peers, their word knowledge appears to develop somewhat differently (Anderson & Reilly, 2002). Further, differences in the size and structure of the lexicons for signed and spoken/printed languages may well create challenges to deaf learners' transition from signing to reading (Mayer & Wells, 1996; McEvoy et al., 1999).

Research of this sort is important because vocabulary is a significant predictor of reading comprehension in hearing students (Adams, 1990; Dickinson, Anastasopoulos, McCabe, Peisner-Feinberg, & Poe, 2003) and in deaf students (Garrison, Long, & Dowaliby, 1997; Harris & Beech, 1998; Kelly, 1996; Kyle & Harris, 2006). Unfortunately, deaf students often have been found to have lower vocabulary skills than hearing age-mates. The size of their vocabulary tends to be smaller, the rate in which they acquire new vocabulary is lower, and they less easily develop new word meaning acquisition processes (Geers & Moog, 1989; Lederberg, 2003; Lederberg & Spencer, 2001; Paul, 2003; Waters & Doehring, 1990). Several researchers have pointed out that early identification of hearing loss has a positive effect on vocabulary development (Lederberg, 2003; Prezbindowski & Lederberg, 2003; Yoshinaga-Itano, 2003), presumably the result of early intervention services providing support for both language and cognitive development.

We also can see the literacy challenges created by a lack of associative connections at a higher level of analysis. Wauters et al. (in preparation), for example, found that deaf students' likelihood of making inferences was relatively limited not only in print (see Strassman, 1997, for a review), but also in Sign Language. Deaf and hearing college students were compared on answering factual and inferential questions about written, signed, or spoken passages. Students each read two passages. The deaf students watched two other passages presented via sign and the hearing students saw two passages presented via spoken English. Independent of whether a text was read or watched (in ASL or spoken language), deaf students scored lower than hearing students. The hearing students performed at the same level, overall, in reading and in listening, while the deaf students performed the same overall in reading and in watching sign. For both groups factual questions were easier than inferential questions independent of whether a text was read or watched in ASL or spoken language. However, the difference was slightly larger for deaf students (56% versus 71%) than for hearing students (71% versus 83%). Also, for the deaf students, the difference between the two question types was caused by a difference in ASL only. They answered factual questions after a passage was presented in ASL just as well as the hearing students answered them after a passage was presented in spoken or written language. Answering inferential questions after an ASL passage was harder for deaf students than answering them after reading a text. Apparently, deaf students' receiving information in Sign Language, relative to print, facilitates their comprehension or retrieval of explicit information after the fact, but not their processing of implicit information.

Several other studies have examined deaf students' Sign Language comprehension in the classroom, and several have contrasted natural Sign Languages with English transliteration, simultaneous communication, or spoken language alone (e.g., Cokely, 1990; Jacobs, 1977; Kurz, 2004; Livingston, Singer, & Abramson, 1994; Marschark, Sapere, et al., 2004, 2005; Murphy & Fleischer, 1977). In all of these studies that have included hearing comparison groups, deaf students scored significantly lower on tests of comprehension and learning relative to hearing peers, even when prior knowledge was controlled. Insofar as neither language modality, parental hearing status, nor language background/proficiency have been found to be consistently related to comprehension in those studies, it appears that the situation is more complex than may have been assumed previously and not necessarily specific to literacy, language, or even hearing loss. Yet recent findings indicate that deaf students can learn as much as hearing peers when they have skilled instructors who are sensitive to the knowledge and learning strategies of deaf learners (Marschark, Sapere, et al., 2008).

Conclusions

A large portion of the effort devoted to improving deaf children's literacy has gone into trying to teach them the skills and strategies that work for hearing children, even though it is apparent that deaf and hearing children often have very different background knowledge and learning strategies. Obviously, this approach has not worked very well, and most deaf children still progress far more slowly than hearing children in learning to read, regardless of their preferred language modality and whether or not they have a cochlear implant. This means that deaf students leaving school are at a relatively greater disadvantage, lagging farther behind hearing peers, than when they entered. At the same time, there are clearly many deaf adults and children who are excellent readers and writers.

The literature concerning deaf children's reading skills indicates that while deaf children of deaf parents have been shown to be better readers than deaf children of hearing parents in some studies, others have shown no difference. Indeed, regardless of whether their parents are deaf or hearing, deaf children who are better readers turn out to be the ones who had their hearing losses diagnosed earlier, had early access to fluent language (via Sign Language or spoken language), and were exposed to both Sign Language and English. At the same time, having a mother who is a good signer appears to be more important than whether she is deaf or hearing or the precise age at which a child learns to sign, as long as it is early (Akamatsu et al., 2000; Strong & Prinz, 1997).

If deaf students' reading difficulties are not the result of any particular orientation in their early language experience, early Sign Language can provide most deaf children with earlier access to the world. There does not appear to be any evidence to suggest that learning to sign early interferes with the development of spoken language, and the reverse appears to be true, even for children with cochlear implants. Sign languages have not yet been shown sufficient to provide effective bridges to print literacy (Mayer & Wells, 1996), but early access to language through signing or speech is necessary for providing children with a context for acquiring the cognitive tools that will, in turn, contribute to language development as well as literacy and other domains of academic achievement.

Most globally, it appears that we may be devoting so much time and energy to teaching fundamental skills underlying reading, that we may be overlooking the goals of reading. Most educators acknowledge that we have made relatively little progress in advancing deaf students' print literacy skills, despite decades of trying. To the extent that recent findings concerning deaf students' learning via Sign Language and real-time text indicate that neither of these provides full access in the classroom, it clearly is time to approach the education of deaf students from a new and different tack. That approach has to be an objective one, letting go of assumptions and philosophical biases. It also has to be an empirically-driven one, building on what works and perhaps re-examining methods previously abandoned because of our obsession with literacy as both the barrier and the solution.

References

Adams, M. J. (1990). *Beginning to read: thinking and learning about print.* Cambridge, MA: Massachusetts Institute of Technology.

Akamatsu, C.T., Musselman, C., & Zweibel, A. (2000). Nature vs. Nurture in the development of cognition in deaf people. In P. Spencer, C. Erting, & M. Marschark (Eds.), *Development in context: The deaf children in the family and at school* (pp. 255-274). Mahwah, NJ: Lawrence Erlbaum Associates.

Anderson, D. & Reilly, J. (2002). The Macarthur Communicative Development Inventory: Normative data for American Sign Language. *Journal of Deaf Studies and Deaf Education, 7*, 83-106.

Antia, S. (2007). Can deaf and hard of hearing students be successful in general education classrooms? *TCRecord*, www.tcrecord.org/PrintContent.asp?ContentID=13461 Retrieved May 17, 2007.

Arnold, P., Palmer, C. & Lloyd, J. (1999). Hearing-impaired children's listening skills in a referential communication task: An exploratory study. *Deafness and Education International, 1*, 47-55.

Bebko, J.M. & Metcalfe-Haggert, A. (1997). Deafness, language skills, and rehearsal: A model for the development of a memory strategy. *Journal of Deaf Studies and Deaf Education, 2*, 131-139.

Cokely, D. (1990). The effectiveness of three means of communication in the college classroom. *Sign Language Studies, 69*, 415-439.

Dickinson, D. K., Anastasopoulos, L., McCabe, A., Peisner-Feinberg, E.S., & Poe, M. D. (2003). The comprehensive language approach to early literacy: The interrelationships among vocabulary, phonological sensitivity, and print knowledge among preschool-aged children. *Journal of Educational Psychology, 95*, 465-381.

Dye, M., Hauser, P., & Bavelier, D. (2008). Visual Attention in deaf children and adults: Implications for learning environments. In M. Marschark & P. Hauser, *Deaf cognition: Foundations and outcomes* (pp. 250-263). New York: Oxford University Press.

Garrison, W., Long, G., & Dowaliby, F. (1997). Working memory capacity and comprehension processes in deaf readers. *Journal of Deaf Studies and Deaf Education, 2,* 78-94.

Geers, A. E., & Moog, J. S. (1989). Factors predictive of the development of literacy in hearing-impaired adolescents. *Volta Review, 91*, 69-86.

Harris, M. & Beech, J. (1998). Implicit phonological awareness and early reading development in prelingually deaf children. *Journal of Deaf Studies and Deaf Education, 3*, 205-216.

Jacobs, L.R. (1977). The efficiency of interpreting input for processing lecture information by deaf college students. *Journal of Rehabilitation of the Deaf, 11*, 10-14.

Kelly, L. (1996). The interaction of syntactic competence and vocabulary during reading by deaf students. *Journal of Deaf Studies and Deaf Education, 1,* 76-90.

Kurz, K. B. (2004). *A comparison of deaf children's learning in direct communication versus an interpreted environment.* Unpublished doctoral dissertation, University of Kansas, Lawrence.

Kyle, F. E. & Harris, M. (2006). Concurrent correlates and predictors of reading and spelling achievement in deaf and hearing school children. *Journal of Deaf Studies and Deaf Education, 11*, 273-288.

Lang, H.G., Dowaliby, F.J., & Anderson, H. (1994). Critical teaching incidents: Interviews with deaf college students. *American Annals of the Deaf, 139*, 119-127.

Lang, H.G., McKee, B.G., & Connor, K.N. (1993). Characteristics of effective teachers: A descriptive study of perceptions of faculty and deaf college students. *American Annals of the Deaf, 138*, 252-259.

Lederberg, A. R. (2003). Expressing meaning: From communicative intent to building a lexicon. In M. Marschark & P. E. Spencer, *Oxford handbook of deaf studies, language, and education* (pp. 247-260). New York: Oxford University Press.

Lederberg, A. R., & Spencer, P. E. (2001). Vocabulary development of deaf and hard of hearing children. In M. D. Clark, M. Marschark, & M. Karchmer (Eds.), *Context, cognition, and deafness* (pp. 88-112). Washington, DC: Gallaudet University Press.

Leigh, G. R. & Power, D. J. (1998, August). Communicating with deaf students: Does simultaneous communication inhibit the development of oral skills? Paper presented at *6th Asia-Pacific Congress on Deafness*, Beijing, China.

Livingston, S., Singer, B., & Abramson, T. (1994). A study to determine the effectiveness of two different kinds of interpreting. *Proceedings of the Tenth National Convention of the Conference of Interpreter Trainers - Mapping our course: A collaborative venture*, pp. 175-197. Sacramento, CA: CIT.

Lloyd, J., Lieven, E., & Arnold, P. (2005). The oral referential communication skills of hearing-impaired children. *Deafness and Education International, 7*, 22-42.

Long, G.L. & Beil, D.H. (2005). The importance of direct communication during continuing education workshops for deaf and hard-of-hearing professionals. *Journal of Postsecondary Education and Disability, 18*, 5-11.

Marschark, M., Convertino, C., & LaRock, D. (2006). Optimizing academic performance of deaf students: Access, opportunities, and outcomes. In D. F. Moores & D. S. Martin (Eds.), *Deaf learners: New developments in curriculum and instruction* (pp. 179-200). Washington, DC: Gallaudet University Press.

Marschark, M., Leigh, G., Sapere, P., Burnham, D., Convertino, C., Stinson, M., Knoors, H., Vervloed, M. P. J. & Noble, W. (2006). Benefits of Sign Language interpreting and text alternatives to classroom learning by deaf students. *Journal of Deaf Studies and Deaf Education, 11*, 421-437.

Marschark, M., Pelz, J., Convertino, C., Sapere, P., Arndt, M. E., & Seewagen, R. (2005). Classroom interpreting and visual information processing in mainstream education for deaf students: Live or Memorex?® *American Educational Research Journal, 42*, 727-762.

Marschark, M., Sapere, P., Convertino, C.M. & Pelz, J. (2008). Learning via direct and mediated instruction by deaf students. *Journal of Deaf Studies and Deaf Education*.

Marschark, M., Sapere, P., Convertino, C., & Seewagen, R. (2005). Access to postsecondary education through Sign Language interpreting. *Journal of Deaf Studies and Deaf Education, 10*, 38-50.

Marschark, M., Sapere, P., Convertino, C., Seewagen, R. & Maltzan, H. (2004). Comprehension of Sign Language interpreting: deciphering a complex task situation. *Sign Language Studies, 4*, 345-368.

Mayer, C. & Wells, G. (1996). Can the linguistic interdependence theory support a bilingual-bicultural model of literacy education for deaf students? *Journal of Deaf Studies and Deaf Education, 1*, 93-107.

McEvoy, C., Marschark, M., & Nelson, D. L. (1999). Comparing the mental lexicons of deaf and hearing individuals. *Journal of Educational Psychology, 91*, 1-9.

Moeller, M. P. (2000). Early intervention and language development in children who are deaf and hard of hearing. *Pediatrics, 106* (3), 1-9.

Murphy, H.J. & Fleischer, L.R. (1977). The effects of Ameslan versus Siglish upon test scores. *Journal of Rehabilitation of the Deaf, 11*, 15-18.

Paul, P. V. (2003). Processes and components of reading. In M. Marschark & P. E. Spencer, *Oxford handbook of deaf studies, language, and education* (pp. 97-109). New York: Oxford University Press.

Prezbindowski, A. K., & Lederberg, A. R. (2003). Vocabulary assessment of deaf and hard-of-hearing children from infancy through the preschool years. *Journal of Deaf Studies and Deaf Education, 8*, 383-400.

Strassman, B. K. (1997). Metacognition and reading in children who are deaf: A review of the research. *Journal of Deaf Studies and Deaf Education, 2,* 140-149.

Strong, M. & Prinz, P.M. (1997). A study of the relationship between American Sign Language and English literacy. *Journal of Deaf Studies and Deaf Education, 2*, 37-46.

Waters, G., & Doehring, P. G. (1990). Reading acquisition in congenitally deaf children who communicate orally. In T. Carr & B. Levy (Eds.), *Reading and its development: Component skills approaches* (pp. 323-373). London: Academic Press.

Wauters, L. N., van Bon, W. H. J., & Tellings, A. E. J. M. (2006). Reading comprehension of Dutch deaf children. *Reading and Writing: An Interdisciplinary Journal, 19*, 49-76.

Yoshinaga-Itano, C. (2003). From screening to early identification and intervention: Discovering predictors to successful outcomes for children with significant hearing loss. *Journal of Deaf Studies and Deaf Education, 8*, 11-30.

Summary of the conference discussion

The discussions around this paper started with a thread on teachers, with one delegate asking: "Given that there is no discreet provision for deaf students in higher education in the UK, and deaf students are always a minority in any student group, I fear that they will never get the benefit that a good teacher could bring. Did the presenters find there were significant differences between learning in deaf students in smaller groups? Were there differences between deaf-only classes and mainstream?"

The experiments for these research studies were done in controlled settings, all of the lectures and interpretations were video taped so that each group of students saw the exact same thing. No real classrooms were used and some of the groups were very small, 1 or 2 students, others were as many as 10.

Other delegates shared their experiences of teaching deaf students. One questioned the efficacy of smaller, contained class sizes. Theoretically this means that teachers have a chance to meet the needs of each student in the classroom. But what does a small class size do to the breadth of knowledge brought to classroom discussions? In larger class sizes of twenty, hearing students can learn from each other and get the benefit of each others' input. What happens though when we reduce this class size for Deaf and hard of hearing children in order to have more one-on-one instruction from the teacher? What does that do to the dynamic in the classroom? How do these students learn to gain insight from their peers if there are only three of them?

Similarly, do deaf learners prefer to be taught by deaf tutors? For example, many deaf learners say that being taught English by a Deaf tutor through Sign Language makes it far easier for them to grasp and understand. This may be due to the way the teachers explain concepts, making them clearer and more geared towards BSL understanding, than a hearing tutor who is interpreted with their audience being primarily hearing. Are Deaf tutors better equipped to teach deaf students language?

Anecdotally, students do report preferring direct teaching in Sign Language to an interpreted English class, but it is difficult to assess if this is because of the accuracy of the interpretation, or because the course is tailored to meet the needs of deaf learners.

Using teachers skilled in English and Sign Language, who can teach English as a second language, building on the grammar knowledge in sign, would seem to be most efficient, but most deaf students and pupils are not being taught English as a second language. They are being taught using the methodology that goes with teaching it as the primary language. There are some instances in the UK where English is being taught to Deaf students as a second language and this means that the students can underpin what they are learning with their existing knowledge of BSL. Although this system might appear to work better, it still presupposes that the Deaf students have a good knowledge of their native Sign Language, and sometimes this is not the case as it is not generally taught as a subject in school and many Deaf people pick it up informally and therefore don't explicitly know how the language works.

From the presenter's research involving college students, they found no differences in learning as a function whether instructors were deaf or hearing, signing for themselves, using interpreters, or using different modes of signed communication. What seems to be essential is how deaf students learn, what they know, and how to optimise their access. Teachers like that normally are signers themselves, but there appear to be no significant differences between signing students and oral students.

With regard to those students who are signers, the researchers observed instructors with better and worse sign skills who are equally effective as teachers because they understand and know how to "communicate" with deaf learners. This is the important factor. A person with excellent sign skills is not necessarily a quality teacher. Just because someone is a skilled signer or deaf does not make them a good teacher for deaf students.

So what is it that makes an excellent teacher? One suggestion was that an excellent teacher figures out where the child is and what he needs to know next and brings him to that 'next' level. The ability to communicate in the language understood by the child is a given, and it doesn't matter what the modality is, as long as the child has access to 100 % of it, but the art involves how to diagnose what the child knows and then figure out how to get him to the next level. It is worth remembering that all children do not learn the same – 'one size fits all' never works.

The paper mentioned that even if the vocabulary bases of deaf and hearing children are similar, their word knowledge develops in different ways, and that this knowledge is organised differently in the two populations. While there are signs for many concepts, it is not as easy for deaf children to acquire the numerous meanings/signs/applications for particular words. With fewer opportunities for incidental learning, it takes more deliberate effort from parents and teachers to ensure that children are exposed to the range of meanings and nuances that will support comprehension in Sign Language and print.

Most deaf children have hearing parents which makes language quite inaccessible if the parents do not know Sign Language. Apart from that, if parents have learned Sign Language, information from the outside world is only available to the deaf child if someone provides the information in Sign Language. They will not learn anything from conversations other people have or from television programmes (captioning is only useful when the child can read). This limited access to language results in fewer opportunities to expand the vocabulary level, especially when language is needed to understand the information around you. The presenters have found that even word meanings that can be learned mainly through perceptual information (as opposed to through language) are difficult for deaf children to learn, probably because they miss a lot of the extra information hearing children acquire through incidental learning.

For hearing children, most vocabulary learning from the age of 8 years on occurs through reading. For most deaf children this is a challenge because their reading level is low. In the early years it is important that parents read to their children. Children learn a lot from this process: they learn about books, they learn about written language and its functions, they start to realise that their parents are not just making up stories but do something with the letters in the book, they learn knew words. Indeed, reading to your child in Sign Language is different than in spoken language, but as long as the language is accessible to the child, s/he will learn a lot from reading together. Important in reading to children is repetition: through repetition they learn more and more about the concepts. Increasing their vocabulary is not more difficult for deaf children because of the use of Sign Language or fingerspelling, but because they do not seem to have the same opportunities as hearing children have. Indeed, linking the sign to the fingerspelled word and to the printed word is a strategy that is often used in vocabulary instruction. By doing this, the child will learn to link these together.

Incidental learning - and the lack thereof - is perhaps the biggest factor, not only for language but for cognitive development, which then drives language acquisition. Parents are key players in this.

Although many hearing parents in newborn hearing screening programmes are advised on cochlear implants more than on Sign Language, if the parents do decide to embrace Sign Language as the best route for their baby they will have to learn to sign themselves. How long does it take to become fluent in Sign Language? How fluent will they be in the grammar and structure? Children need to be exposed not just to vocabulary, but to structure and grammar in order to develop the foundations of language needed. And suppose these well-meaning parents are aware of this, where do they go to find Deaf or fluent hearing signing adults who will spend time with their baby, exposing them to language?

There is some anecdotal and small-sample evidence that parents do not have to be fluent signers of the natural Sign Language for their child to grow up being one. An example is parents who immigrate into the UK from Italy. The parents may still speak Italian, but that does not mean that their children will not grow up fluent in English. The situation is somewhat more complicated for deaf children (and it has been found that there is a relationship between classroom learning and whether there is a third language used in the home beyond English and Sign Language), but studies that show that deaf children of deaf parents do better in schools and deaf children of hearing parents have not isolated Sign Language as the cause. The evidence is very clear that early access to language makes everything go more smoothly (i.e. development, learning, achievement, socialisation, etc.). But hearing parents can do that for their deaf children and the purported advantages for deaf children of deaf parents over deaf children of hearing parents, and least in literacy, are not as clear as many people would claim.

Hearing people often do not state what they actually mean and rely on inference to get their message across. Many Sign Languages are far more direct. Deaf children may never be taught that they have to 'read between the lines' (in both print and sign). Do they know that the information they get is not always complete and that they have to infer some of the information from what is said explicitly? This is a part of metacognition that should get attention in education. This may be related to the Theory of Mind as well as metacognition differences in deaf people. For example, the ability to think about not only what you are going to say to another person, but also how that person might perceive what you say, and how that perception may vary depending on how the information is communicated (words, intent, expression, etc.). Teachers need to understand the Theory of Mind with regard to how children are seeing/interpreting the world.

One delegate shared her experience: "My experience has been that not only are children unaware they might need to "read between the lines" but they may also lack the confidence in even knowing they are allowed to do so! Many of the Deaf/HH children I've worked with seem to need to hear from an adult that it's OK to question what people mean. Mostly if students hear/see something, they are used to feeling like the speaker/signer has more knowledge and they don't like to admit that they may not agree with the outright meaning of a message. Teaching them that this is not only applicable to academics but everyday living is essential! It relates to language development in general as well. Giving students the confidence (through direct teaching) to say "I'm not sure I understand the message" will help them search for answers, and thus language. It also forces the speaker/signer to be more clear, choose different words or signs to express the same concept and thus leads to greater exposure and more connections. Knowing the difference between "I don't understand" and "I don't agree with the meaning" is crucial and knowing how to handle each is even more important."

Most deaf college students show remarkable communication flexibility. Data over the past 6 years has been remarkably consistent in showing that there are not only issues of communication differences but in cognitive processing of information as well. We continually talk about deaf students underperforming compared to their hearing peers. If they are truly their peers, we would not be comparing them to monolingual hearing students. Has there been a comparison between deaf students' struggle and that of other English as a foreign language learners?

The presenter team have compared college deaf students to international students who are English second language users. While the results are interesting, it still seems like an unfair comparison as the international students have a strong first language other than English. While it does seem that comparing deaf students to hearing students is unfair, they are in an "educational system" that does indeed compare all students to each other. There has long been the illusion that inclusion and mainstreaming, i.e. that providing access services like interpreters, has indeed provided full access to deaf students in the classroom. In fact the word "equal" access is used to describe such a setting. Part of the goal of the research is to point out that clearly there is not equal access in the classroom. If there was, deaf students as a whole would not be performing consistently below their hearing age equivalent classmates. In order to be able to teach deaf children it is important to know where they differ, so we are able to accommodate.

Boundary Issues in Educational Interpreting: Where do You Draw the Line?
by Richard Brumberg

Introduction

In a typical public school classroom, the roles of the professionals are clearly defined. Even as young as five years old, a new student learns very quickly that the teacher's rules are the law. This adult will impart and reinforce concepts and techniques necessary for the student to use throughout his/her educational career and, in turn, his/her life. The teacher will also assess the student's work as well as monitor his/her behaviour in the classroom. Furthermore, the student knows s/he can give feedback sometimes, particularly about his/her progress during class. (e.g.: "What does [word] mean?"; "I've learned about black holes before"; "I don't get what you're saying.")

The classroom may also include a paraprofessional, or para-pro, especially in the younger grades or inclusion classrooms. The para-pro does not determine what will be taught and how it will be taught. S/he is not responsible for tabulating a student's final grade. However, s/he still has authority over the students' behaviour and, often times, is left in charge of the class when the teacher leaves the room or is absent.[1]

What happens, then, when an American Sign Language (ASL)/spoken English educational interpreter becomes part of the classroom milieu? Often, the consumers (both hearing and Deaf/hard of hearing (HoH)) have little, if any experience working with the

---

[1] There are many other professionals that the student encounters every day- the principal, assistant principal, school nurse, guidance counselor, etc. For the purpose of this paper, however, we will focus on those present for the majority of the student's time in the classroom.

interpreter and knowing his/her role.[1] In other instances, the teacher and student may have worked with an interpreter whose role was ill-defined.

To make things more complicated, the interpreter may have beliefs that appear to contradict each other. Interpreters often say there must be boundaries in this setting. Almost within the same breath, though, they'll say positive rapport and being part of the educational team are paramount for a successfully interpreted environment. Feeling stymied, the interpreter may be unable to say anything about his/her role at all. At best, s/he may resort to hiding behind the "I'm just the interpreter" or NOT-MY-BUSINESS responses.[2] These statements or actions may undermine the establishment of positive relationships with the Deaf student and educational team.

This brings us to the central question of this paper: What is the balance between establishing healthy relationships and keeping your distance in the educational arena? Should interpreters draw boundaries and if so, what kind of line should they be? This paper will explore this issue and offer possible solutions through a synthesis of established research and first-person experiences/responses. It suggests that the interpreter's two beliefs may be able to co-exist if the boundary is in the right place and has the right flexibility. The paper will also focus on the language interpreters use and how word choice has a profound effect on creating and maintaining healthy and professional relationships in the classroom.

The Geography of Boundaries

According to the Encarta Dictionary, the word boundary has two definitions. It can mean a "border" or "the official line that divides one area of land from another".[3] For example, the walls of an

---

[1] Note: For the sake of brevity, the word "Deaf" will stand for both Deaf and Hard of Hearing individuals.
[2] Note: Words in all capital letters are glosses for ASL signs. Words with hyphens are the equivalent of one sign. Where necessary, a translation will be included.
[3] "boundary." *Encarta Dictionary: English (North America)*. 2008. Microsoft Word (January 11, 2008).

apartment make the boundary between space that one person pays and what his/her neighbour pays. It can also describe a "limit" as in "the point at which something ends or beyond which it becomes something else".[1] For instance, when a child starts to colour a clown's nose, s/he is instructed to stay within the lines. If s/he doesn't, s/he'll be colouring another part of the clown.

Boundaries are often set to show clarification and employ protection. Think of how confusing or dangerous a soccer match might be if there were no white lines on the field. The players wouldn't be able to identify the goals or they could run into a wall. Consider, as well, a highway with no lines. Drivers would not be able to stay in a lane; there would be no consistent place to turn or get on or off. If there was no median or divider, drivers would not know whether they were coming or going! The divider is the boundary between west-bound and east-bound traffic.

In this sense, when we talk about educational interpreting, boundaries are meant to be safeguards for all of the stakeholders- the Deaf student, the classroom teacher and the interpreter. There are also stakeholders who are not immediately present but still vital to the educational environment. For example, Conrad and Stegenga suggest that parents of Deaf children may "rely on interpreter rather than the teacher as the expert on Deaf children" and that this may "inadvertently creat[e] role conflicts within the classroom."[2] A boundary of role responsibilities would help clarify this situation.

In a series of interviews conducted with Deaf consumers, a classroom teacher and working educational interpreters, there was agreement that boundaries were necessary for an interpreted environment. They cited different kinds of boundaries. For example, one interpreter said that there was a boundary as to how much one needed to know about the student's makeup and would "only check personal information about [the student's] educational background and language."[3] This interpreter also stated that, when you see the student for the first time in class, you only need to talk "pleasantries"

---

[1] Ibid.
[2] Conrad and Stegenga, 2005, p. 298.
[3] Personal interview, 2008. (Note: Unless otherwise stated, quotes in this paper come from these interviews conducted in 2008.

and you "don't need to be socializing" with the student. When asked what to say to a student who came back after being sick, a response might be " 'Welcome back. We missed you.' but nothing more than that."

For one of the Deaf consumers, thinking back on interpreted high school and university classrooms, it was appreciated when the interpreter would "act *like* the teacher but not *be* the teacher." This was done "through facial expressions and mannerisms". This boundary serves two purposes. Linguistically, it shows who is speaking (and who is not speaking). It also shows that the teacher is running the class and not the interpreter.

Another Deaf consumer, who is also a Deaf interpreter, offers an additional example of a healthy boundary. When asked what it was like to work with CODAs (Children of Deaf Adults), the consumer stated that there was a big difference between a CODA who went through an interpreter training program (ITP) and one who did not attend. Individuals who did graduate from a program were more professional. They "had that boundary and had ethics that what we said [during the assignment] would not be passed around the community". In this case, there are ethical and spatial boundaries that dictate what can be said during an assignment and what can be discussed with the general public.

The above examples are all crucial for interpreted environments- particularly in the educational settings with young Deaf children. When there are no set boundaries, these students will not be able to "distinguish between a teacher and an interpreter- all [they] see is a 'big person' ".[1] In fact, one resource about educational interpreting considers "professional boundaries and behaviour from the interpreter" to be part of the "Student's Bill of Rights". [2] Moreover, educational interpreters work in the same classroom on an on-going basis. The way things are set in the beginning is more than likely the way it'll be throughout the school year.

---

[1] Humphrey and Alcorn. 1995, p 299.
[2] Schick. *Classroom Interpreting*.
http;//www.classroominterpreting.org/Students?StudentsRights.asp. Retrieved January 2, 2008.

Standards and Boundaries: Bridging the "Yes" with the "No"

In all of the previous examples, there is a sense of prohibition - i.e. I *can't* talk to you about this; those are the teacher's words and *not* mine; this will *not* be discussed outside of this classroom. This is part of what makes novice interpreters hesitant; they want to set the boundaries with the consumers without damaging any rapport. We might want take a cue from other business practices and how they deal with boundaries. Thomas J. Leonard, who uses coaching as a way to succeed in business and in personal growth, comments that many professionals lump standards and boundaries together, calling them all boundaries. He makes a marked distinction between these two ideas. While boundaries are "what you have determined that other people or environments cannot do TO you", standards "are the behaviours/excellence that you naturally hold yourself to". [1] As stated above, we talk about boundaries in terms of "No". When we think about setting standards, we use the idea of "Yes" and what I *can and will* do to make teaching and learning achievable.

This is not to imply that boundaries are bad and standards are good. In reality, these two go together. For instance, according to Schick, "the classroom teacher is responsible for the discipline in his/her classroom- for all of the students, not just the ones who can hear." She also says it is critical for the interpreter and teacher to communicate how they will deal with discipline issues.[2] The teacher and interpreter, working as a team, could establish the standard that the interpreter will point out a behaviour if it's disrupting the interpreting process since facilitating communication is his/her priority. The teacher will carry out the discipline and be responsible for all other behaviours. Furthermore, they could add that if there is an emergency, the interpreter would be more than willing to step in and give a hand. If the two adults agree to this and are each consistent, the standards will create a natural boundary. The students

---

[1] Leonard. The Top 10 Keys to Understanding Boundaries and Standards. *Coachville Coach Training Resource Center*. http://www.topten.org/public/bj/bj28.html. pp 1-2. Retrieved January 2, 2008.

[2] Schick. Regular Education Teachers- Discipline and the Educational Interpreter. *Classroom Interpreting*. http://www.classroominterpreting.org/Teachers/discipline.asp. Retrieved January 2, 2008.

will learn where something won't happen by always going to where it does happen.[1] As one interpreter interviewed put it, "The kids need to know who's boss."

As a word of caution, though, Leonard suggests that there is a boundary and standard "trap".[2] If we are not careful, we will only focus on the boundaries and standards without looking at the big picture. For educational interpreting, the overall goals are for the Deaf student to understand what's going on in the classroom (and feel that s/he is a part of the class) and for the teacher to monitor what and how much the students have learned (and that the Deaf student is a part of the class). If the standards and boundaries do not help these overriding goals, the standards and boundaries we are using are empty and serve no purpose.

For instance, the Registry of Interpreters for the Deaf's/National Association of the Deaf's Code of Professional Conduct (CPC) says that "[i]nterpreters adhere to the standards of confidential communication".[3] An educational interpreter may misinterpret this to mean as not being allowed to tell anyone about what happens in the classroom. However, if a teacher and student work with more than one interpreter throughout the day, the interpreters must be able to communicate to each other what is happening in the classroom. This form of open communication would not violate the CPC guideline. In reality, it will help maintain consistency which will indeed further the overall goals.

The Thickest Boundary

Having said this, one may wonder if there are any boundaries in educational interpreting that are fixed; they can never be relaxed or erased. If there are such boundaries, what boundary would be the

---

[1] This is just like a basketball game. Players will not try for a foul shot from their team's bench because they are always directed to stand on the foul line. This creates a boundary on the court between where they can and can't play the game.
[2] Leonard. p 2. Retrieved January 2, 2008.
[3] Code of Professional Conduct. *Ethics.* http://www.rid.org/ethics/code/index.cfm. Retrieved December 27, 2007.

strongest? To arrive at an answer, the participants were asked to consider the ideal relationship between:

- the Deaf student and the interpreter
- the teacher and the Deaf student
- the teacher and the interpreter.

While there was some variation, in almost all of the responses, there was a belief that the teacher and interpreter needed to have open communication in order to delegate the roles and responsibilities of each person. This approach helps establish an atmosphere of teamwork. One consumer suggested that the interpreter and teacher could meet before school started so they would be able to "predict each other's skills". They would be able to delineate between the interpreter's and the teacher's roles. They could work out the kinks instead of being faced with it in the midst of instruction. It would also be beneficial to revisit this discussion throughout the year. (One interpreter reported that after having several lengthy discussions with the classroom teacher, the two of them developed shorthand of communication and giving feedback during class because their thought processes were synchronised.)

Another interpreter differentiated an aspect between the interpreter's role and the teacher's role this way: "The teacher has a mixture of hearing and Deaf children. They are experts on children. We [interpreters] are experts on the language of their Deaf children."

This is a powerful statement. It shows a more global demarcation between the teacher's and interpreter's roles and is a good rule of thumb when thinking about who should give what information. For example, at an annual IEP (Individual Educational Program) meeting when the team asks about the Deaf student's progress, the teacher could talk about the Deaf student's math scores. The interpreter, in kind, could talk about how the student has mastered an aspect of ASL like the contrastive structure.[1]

---

[1] Contrastive structure is when two entities (people, places, ideas, etc.) are established as points in space- ex. comparing addition with subtraction and placing addition to the left of the signer and subtraction to the right. These references remain in space and the signer always shifts signs to one area when s/he's detailing that entity.

These comments reflect one boundary that must remain fixed: the boundary between the teacher's role and the interpreter's role. It helps maintain clarity for all involved- especially the Deaf student. In fact, one major complaint from Deaf consumers was how interpreters become too involved or controlling. One Deaf consumer, reflecting on her educational experience so far, says in general "interpreters are wonderful for when you're trying to deal with hearing people... [My interpreters] would help me with homework and chat with me when there was no instruction."[1] On the other hand, some interpreters "were overly controlling and would keep telling me not to do things. I don't think that's right. The interpreter's there to hear what the teacher says and sign it. S/he's not supposed to control behaviour. *That's the teacher's job, not the interpreter's.*"[2]

This kind of behaviour is what strains these relationships. It is not that the student thinks she should be allowed to misbehave. It is the act of the interpreter telling her not to do something that violates the standards set by the roles. She expects reprimands from the teacher and not the interpreter. In the same vein, a teacher may view this as the interpreter usurping his/her role as disciplinarian or might start expecting the interpreter to behave like a para-pro.[3] By upholding the standards, the boundaries stay in place.

Language in Action: How to Make it Work

In theory, all of this sounds appealing. However, building the rapports and setting the standards is a continuous balancing act for the interpreter. Two salient features of a skilled interpreter are the direct word choice and actions used when dealing with consumers.

---

[1] Rita. (2007, December 15). My experience with interpreters. *Wordpress.com: Rita's Expressive Vlog*. Retrieved January 2, 2008 from
http://chillygurlz.wordpress.com/2007/12/15/my-experience-with-interpreters.
2 Ibid. Italics mine.
3 Going back to the soccer analogy, it would be like the referee blocking a kick and preventing a goal. The players would not be mad about a block; that's part and parcel of the game. They would be furious that a referee started playing. That action violates the boundary between the referee's and the opposing player's functions.

This could concern how we name ourselves and our relationship to the students.[1] It also deals with our exact responses to certain instances in the classroom.

Many seasoned interpreters perform these skills so well that they may not even realise how they are doing it. Therefore, several scenarios were devised for the working interpreters interviewed. A situation was given and then the interpreters were asked exactly what they would sign or say (depending, naturally, if a Deaf or hearing consumer initiated the conversation).

In one situation, a 7th grader (12-13 years old) is given a review sheet about the planets and is told to work independently. He asks the interpreter G+R+A+V+I+T+Y, WHAT MEAN? Almost all of the interpreters assumed that a sign had already been established and they would first give that sign. When asked why, many interpreters echoed this interpreter's response: "I'm trying to figure out if it [the question] is related to the English word or the concept." If the student still said he didn't understand, the interpreters would give answers like COME-ALONG ASK-TO TEACHER? or WHY-NOT YOU-ME, ASK TEACHER and G+R+A+V+I+T+Y THAT ONE YOUR WORDS RIGHT? YOU RAISE-HAND ASK TEACHER. I ADMIT INTERPRET.[2] Another option was to start voicing right to the teacher and letting them mediate the situation.

When the interpreters were asked why the response was another question or why the signs ADMIT and WHY-NOT were used, the interpreters responded with ideas like "It's a gentle push out of the nest. [It's a p]rompt to the student that I'm here to interpret for [him]," and "It's up to the student if...[he] wants to ask the teacher. I don't want to demand...[him]." This approach cushions and protects the relationship between the Deaf student and the interpreter. Just answering with "It's not my responsibility" leaves the Deaf student rattled. One Deaf consumer did not have an interpreter until he graduated from the school for the Deaf and went to college. He

---

[1] Coon, J. and Brumberg, R. "Whose Student?", *VIEWS*, December, 2007, 24(11), 8,21.
[2] "Hey, do you want to ask the teacher about that word?" or "Why don't you and I go up to the teacher and you can ask him." and "Isn't that a word from your list? If you raise your hand and ask the teacher, I'd be willing to interpret the conversation."

received the colder response and said he felt embarrassed. One can only imagine the effect that reply would have on a 12 year old.

In another scenario, the teacher asks the interpreter the reading level of the Deaf student. The interpreters answered (with degrees of variation) "I don't know. I'm only familiar with [the Deaf student's] interpreting needs. But [student] is part of [teacher of the Deaf]'s caseload and s/he would have that info for you." When asked why they included information about the teacher of the deaf, one interpreter said that the goal is "to guide [the classroom teacher] to the appropriate person…You're teaching [the teacher]." Another said giving this information is "a way to be helpful for my co-workers. It fosters goodwill between the classroom teacher and the Deaf/Hard of Hearing Department."

Here we see another version of softening the blow. The error is not in the question but in who was asked. Using the word "caseload" is very powerful because it makes that person the repository for the student and lifts this additional responsibility from the interpreter. Once the teacher gets that answer from the case manager, the relationship between the teacher and the interpreter will strengthen. As a veteran classroom teacher put it, "It's important to be able to talk [to the interpreter]. It's not just interpreting." That is, interpreters cannot go into a room blindly and just start interpreting. Open and friendly communication is of utmost importance.

Conclusion

The interpreted classroom is loaded with personalities and behaviours. Boundaries and rapports need to coexist. Without boundaries and standards in place, there would be complete chaos. Moreover, it is the appropriate involvement from the interpreter that keeps the standards in place. The standards help foster positive and professional relationships for all involved in the classroom. In turn, these relationships keep the boundaries in check. When all of this is established, the possibilities for the Deaf child's education are almost limitless.

References

"boundary." *Encarta Dictionary: English (North America)*. 2008. Microsoft Word (January 11, 2008).

Coon, J. and Brumberg, R. (2007, December) "Whose Student?", *VIEWS*.

Humphrey, J. and Alcorn, B. (1995). *So You Want to be an Interpreter? An Introduction to Sign Language Interpreting.* Amarillo, TX: H & H Publishers.

Janzen, T. (Ed.). (2005) *Topics in Signed Language Interpreting.* Philadelphia, PA: John Benjamins.

Leonard, T. (1996) "The Top 10 Keys to Understanding Boundaries And Standards", *Coachville Coach Training Resource Center*. http://www.topten.org/public/bj/bj28.html. Retrieved January 2, 2008.

Personal Communications, January, 2008.

Registry of Interpreters for the Deaf. (2005). NAD-RID Code of Professional Conduct. Retrieved September, 2006 from http://rid.org/codeofethics.pdf

Rita. (2007, December 15). "My experience with interpreters". *Wordpress.com: Rita's Expressive Vlog.* Retrieved January 2, 2008 from http://chillygurlz.wordpress.com/2007/12/15/my-experience-with-interpreters

Schick, B. "Regular Education Teachers - Discipline and the Educational Interpreter". *Classroom Interpreting* http://www.classroominterpreting.org/Teachers/discipline.asp. Retrieved January 2, 2008

Schick, B. "Students- Student's rights regarding interpreters", *Classroom Interpreting.* http;//www.classroominterpreting.org/Students?StudentsRights.asp. Retrieved January 2, 2008.

Summary of the conference discussion

The discussion on this topic began with a question on how it is possible to educate school staff on the role of the interpreter. This would aid in establishing a standard for interpreters which would result in interpreter's boundaries becoming more standardised.

One suggestion was orientations for staff, particularly if it is the first time they have ever had Deaf students and interpreters in the school. One important aspect of this is that it is important for staff and interpreters to meet several times, regularly if possible, to be able to revisit issues again and again. Staff may not know what to expect from interpreters or how to teach a deaf child, so they may need time to be able to find out what questions they should be asking. It is also beneficial for staff to be addressed by a deaf person/professional so that staff can experience a different context (seeing themselves as consumers) of interacting with interpreters. This would also show teachers that the interpreter is not only for the Deaf pupils, but for everyone in the school.

A few carefully thought through language issues can make a difference in defining the difference between the teacher/interpreter role. How an interpreter acts within the physical space can make all the difference on how they are viewed as professionals. For example, it is key on entering the classroom to greet the professor or teacher as a co-worker and indicate by their manner of approach, use of language that this is the professional team the students kids will be engaging with that session? Where the interpreter chooses to place themselves can also make a big difference. Providing clear sight lines to the presentation materials/interpreter/teacher the student is then often free to choose a place away from the front and does not need to spend the lesson seated in very close proximity to an interpreter which can give the impression that the interpreter is there as personal learning assistant instead of a facilitator of bilingual teaching for the tutor and indeed the whole class. It might also be beneficial to mirror the teacher/lecturer's pattern of eye gaze e.g. travelling around the classroom. This might this also have the added benefit of freeing a lone deaf student from any perceived obligation to maintain eye gaze with the interpreter over an extended period of time and give opportunities to dip in and out of full engagement with listening as hearing students are able to?

The physicality of interpreter's work - where they are in relation to the consumers and the material, guiding to make the room as Deaf-friendlly as possible without usurping the teacher's original design, etc.- are part of the standards that help establish an interpreter's role. Even walking in the hallway and entering a classroom speaks volumes about the interpreter's relationship with others around them. For instance, letting the Deaf student knock and/or open the door, or walking beside, not in front of the deaf student.

As for where the student sits, in American public schools, many IEPs (Individual Educational Plans) will list preferential seating as an accommodation. Many people misinterpret this as 'must sit in the front row'. But what is most important is to cut out some of the visual stress for the student and to provide clear sight lines.

The presentation asked the question 'What is the balance between establishing healthy relationships and keeping your distance in the educational area?' One boundary that educational interpreters often cross is the desire to become the helper. When this happens, a common occurrence is when the student needs more clarification on a topic or sentence and the interpreter takes control of the conversation. Rather than the interpreter facilitating the communication between the Deaf student and teacher/peer, the interpreter will provide the clarification. However, students need to experience taking the initiative to seek answers from who ever is available and asking for clarification on their own. This empowerment will assist them with communication barriers throughout their life and provide the opportunity to build self-esteem.

It is important to remember than the boundaries discussed in the paper are primarily those between the teacher and interpreter, rather than the relationship between the Deaf student and the teacher or the Deaf student and the interpreter. There is a difference between boundaries, roles, responsibilities, and best practices. In many educational settings an interpreter must be flexible and a strict interpretation of roles sometimes does not work well in this environment. For example, an interpreter may have a different role working in a high school than in an elementary school.

Younger children will be more dependent on the interpreter as an 'adult', rather than strictly as a professional interpreter. In high school, they will be less dependent and require an interpreter to act within a professional role to facilitate their independence. What makes a successfully mediated classroom has less to do with rigid adherence to roles and boundaries and more to do with the interpreter's ability to discern what is needed and appropriate in any given situation, and strive to meet that need, without fostering unhealthy dependence or sabotaging the system.

However, an interpreter's involvement in a situation is still part of the interpretation. In the paper, the interpreters giving that gentle nudge for the student to direct questions to the teacher, are doing more than being a strict conduit. But once the child understands how it works and whom to direct questions to, the interpreter can put more of the standards described in the paper into the interpretation without having to explain the role again.

Rapport and boundary maintenance are not mutually exclusive and they can co-exist if the boundary is in the right place and has the right flexibility. Often setting boundaries falls on the interpreter because they are, potentially, the only person in the room who knows what everyone's roles are and by establishing boundaries they are just adding one more way, or level, to mediate or help navigate the communication between a deaf person (the student) and a hearing person (the teacher). This other 'level' to the interpreting environment helps the consumers communicate with each other- which is the interpreter's primary purpose for being there. Ideally, it also allows the teacher/student rapport to grow. If the interpreter were to correct the Deaf child's behaviour, the teacher would never be able to assess behaviour levels, nor be aware of improvement. Letting the teacher be involved in discipline lets him/her know what responses work.

Because interpreters are trained to have bilingual/bicultural skills they can communicate with deaf children in a way that other (hearing) people can't. The kids pick up on whether the interpreter is interested or not. If they feel that they are not, then the window of communication will close. If the adults around them feel that the interpreters are too 'separate' from the situation, then the stress level and intensity will mount to an unnecessary level. However, the danger in this is that the student may think the interpreter is the only source of information/support or that the student can only rely on people who can sign. Ideally, interpreters want to be seen as a way to get to the knowledge - not be the source of the knowledge. Their boundaries must not only protect the dignity of the profession, but also provide the greatest quality of service to everyone in the working environment.

Education of the Deaf: Mediated by Interpreters by Patricia Lessard

By definition, Deaf students in the United States fall under the provision of special education. However, they also are required to meet the standards of No Child Left Behind. By and large they are placed in regular education classrooms with support services, in particular, Sign Language interpreters. The key to an effective mainstream education where an interpreter is provided lies in the qualifications of the interpreter. The inclusion of Deaf students in a regular education classroom means that they are in an environment where they do not share the language (in its spoken modality) with the majority of their peers and/or teacher(s). It is the interpreter who must mediate this environment, and as a consequence, mediate their education.

It is hoped that this brief description of recent observations will generate questions as well as encourage discussion about the challenge of training individuals who will eventually work with deaf students in educational environments. The information presented here is from a review of the literature, from data collected over the last 15 years while observing and evaluating students, anecdotal information gathered when speaking with colleagues in other training programs, discussions with peers when working as an interpreter, and comments that have been made during encounters with former students of interpretation who are now working in the field.

No Child Left Behind Act of 2001

To begin, what is the No Child Left Behind Act of 2001? Essentially, the No Child Left Behind Act of 2001[1] (NCLB) is a reauthorisation of the Elementary and Secondary Education Act (ESEA) of 1965.

---

[1] Department of Education, No Child Left Behind:
http://www.ed.gov/nclb/landing.jhtml?src=pb

The Elementary and Secondary Education Act[1] (ESEA) is a United States federal statute which was enacted by President Johnson on April 11, 1965. This statute funds primary and secondary education, basically for students between the ages of five and 18. The ESEA mandates that there must be funds set aside for professional development, instructional materials, resources to support educational programs, and promoting parental involvement. The initial "life-span" of the ESEA was only for five years, until 1970. However the U.S. government, so far, has continued to reauthorise it every five years since its enactment.

The NCLB expands on major reforms proposed by the ESEA, especially state academic standards, student assessment and academic progress, accountability, and school improvement. It has set out several key performance goals for schools and students:

- *All students will be taught by highly qualified teachers by the end of the 2005-06 school year.* Too often, this level of intensive and sustained professional development has not been provided.
- *All students will attain proficiency in reading and mathematics by 2014, including students with disabilities and English learners.* Congress recognised the need for low-achieving children, with limited English proficiency, or disabilities, who need family literacy services.
- *All English learners will become proficient in English.*
- *All students will learn in schools that are safe and drug free.*
- *All students will graduate from high school.* Schools are to provide opportunities for children to acquire knowledge and skills as outlined in the State Content Standards that are set to a challenging level. The students will have access to content that encourages complex thinking and problem-solving skills.

---

[1] Elementary and Secondary Education Act:
www.nea.org/esea/eseabasics.html
www.ed.gov/legislation/ESEA/sec1001.html

In compliance with the goals stated above, local school districts are required to test their students – all students – to ensure that they are making progress in school. The NCLB refers to this progress as "adequate yearly progress" or AYP. Students with disabilities (as deaf students are categorised in the US) are also expected to make AYP. A key factor to consider when measuring the academic progress of any student is their placement in a program that supports students in their development of critical thinking skills, language, and appropriate and meaningful social interactions. With access to the benefits of this type of program, i.e., access that is provided by a qualified interpreter, a deaf student is better positioned for success.

In order for deaf students to acquire literacy skills and to perform at grade level as required by No Child Left Behind, they must have meaningful communication. Communication requires access to the expressed thoughts of the other party in the conversation. In a classroom or other educational setting, this means that the deaf child must have comprehensible input (from the interpreter) in order to understand the message that the teacher or classmates are trying to impart. Comprehension requires that the interpreter provide intelligible output to the student. Intelligible output requires language fluency. The interpreter needs to understand what the teacher is saying. The interpreter needs to be able to convey the content in a way that the deaf student can understand. If the interpreter does not understand the talk of the teacher or other children in the class, then there won't be an accurate interpretation. If the deaf student does not understand the content due to errors or omissions made by the interpreter, then there won't be academic progress. Since the NCLB requires a school to measure a deaf student's academic progress – how can the student be fairly assessed for progress if they aren't getting information in a form that they can access or understand?

Background

With the expectations established by the NCLB Act of 2001, Deaf children in public schools are now faced with the daunting task of performing on par with their hearing peers in all aspects of their academic endeavours. There is a growing concern regarding the education of deaf students that comes to them through interpreters who are not competent to work in an educational setting. Over the last 30 years, more and more deaf students have been placed in mainstreamed settings. According to the 2002 National Center for Educational Statistics, 80% of deaf children in the United States attend local public schools. Placement in an educational institution does not necessarily mean that deaf students will be in an environment where learning takes place for *them*. "Deaf students in mainstream settings are suffering because the interpreters that they have working with them are either not qualified to be working as an interpreter at all, or minimally qualified to be working in an educational setting with young deaf students." (Marshark, 2005) Research on working educational interpreters in the U.S. shows that many do not have language and interpreting skills that are commonly considered as minimum standards in the U.S. Research using the Educational Interpreter Performance Assessment (Schick, Williams, & Bolster, 1999; Schick, Williams, & Kupermintz, 2006) shows that 45% of more than 2,000 interpreters did not have sufficient interpreting skills to be in a classroom.

"An interpreted education seems to place additional demands on [a deaf student's] cognitive processing" (Schick, 2004). The student must coordinate visual attention between the interpreter and other visual information in the classroom, which means that the d/hh [deaf and hard-of-hearing] student likely receives less information than the hearing students (Winston, 2004). The d/hh student also must figure out who is speaking in the classroom in order to make sense of the message (Schick, 2004), a requirement that is challenging to represent for many interpreters (Schick et al., 2006). For their part, educational interpreters are typically second-language learners, so the student must deal with a variety of accents and errors. As we know, the interpretation is likely to be a less rich and complex version of the teacher's communication in addition to being riddled with distortions, errors, and omissions (Langer, 2007), which make learning more challenging. The d/hh student must contend with interpreted communication that is not in synchronisation with what the hearing teacher and peers are doing, pointing, and looking (Winston, 2004). "This short list of increased demands on cognitive resources is clearly incomplete; we really do not know all the factors that may be involved." (Schick, 2008)

Educational Challenges

When deaf children attend a mainstreamed, public school, their success or failure could be the result of the quality of the interpreter employed by the school where they are placed. According to a report on deaf students who were placed in a setting where educational interpreters were employed, published by LaBue (1998), there were five reasons that deaf students gave as to why they have a difficult time following their interpreter:

1. The interpretation, often ungrammatical, and incomprehensible, forced students to depend on their knowledge of English discourse structure and lip reading if they wanted to understand discussions and participate in them.
2. Turn taking in a mainstreamed classroom is usually controlled by auditory cues, which typically don't get (or can't be) interpreted.
3. Many of the cohesive features of spoken English such as repetition, and other discourse markers were not interpreted.
4. Students had a difficult time tracking the topics. They often did not know if the speaker had changed topics or if someone else was talking.
5. Important cues, such as participant relationships and status – ergo the permission to interrupt or not, were not provided.

Qualifications of classroom interpreters vary widely. Based on information gathered from interviews and discussions conducted during my observations and assessments over the years, if there was a spectrum one could use to help categorise the educational interpreters under discussion, they would have been located at any of a number of places. For example, at one end would be an individual who has graduated from an accredited interpreter-training program and who has had years of experience. At the other end are the individuals who have had nothing more than a few Sign Language courses or have learned Sign Language exclusively from a book.

What should be the minimum qualifications of an interpreter? To begin with, one must possess English fluency. Secondly, one must have developed American Sign Language (ASL) fluency. Third, one must have bilingual fluency, i.e., have the aptitude to take the meaning, explicitly stated or implied, from one language and give its appropriate interpretation in the other.

English Fluency

Being fluent in the grammar of English is usually not a problem for interpreters. However, when working in the classroom, they must also recognise different types or genres of discourse in English and what the utterances mean beyond the words in order to effectively convey the intended meaning into ASL. Speakers often use different genres of discourse to achieve particular communicative goals. For example, over the course of a few hours, teacher and students could transition from one genre to another. Their talk could be persuasive, expository, procedural, informational or argumentative in nature. They may be in the middle of a lecture where the teacher describes the process for conducting a lab experiment; perhaps one of the students decides this is the perfect opportunity to argue against genetic testing; the teacher, in turn decides to offer the student advice about seeking or refusing medical interventions, etc. These different ways of speaking will have their own characteristics.

In addition to the genre of the speech, there is the tone that accompanies the words. It can be formal, asserting one's status over the other participant; it can reveal irony or sarcasm, indicate ridicule or judgment, etc. There is also a rising or "checking" intonation in English, which is used by a speaker to see if the listener is able to follow the content of the message. The lack of recognition of these extra-linguistic properties of English has been what caused many of the interpreter errors I observed. As a result, there was confusion and misunderstanding on the part of the student.

Could student struggles be mitigated if the interpreter possessed greater ASL fluency? That is, fluency with the grammar; the ability to recognise the different genres of discourse and provide an equivalent translation that includes the communicative intent of the speaker; and a realisation of the meaning that resides beyond the word level.

ASL Fluency

ASL is a language that is expressed in a modality that differs from the interpreter's spoken language in many ways. It requires years of exposure or training in order to acquire second language (L2) fluency. Acquisition in terms of language refers to the gradual development of ability by using it naturally in communicative situations—long periods spent in social interactions (Yule 1985). As with the young deaf children, such prolonged interactions would allow adult learners to parse the grammar and prosody of ASL into component parts. Once these features have been isolated and identified, they can be rehearsed and successfully incorporated into the interpreted message. There were very few native speakers of ASL in the interpreters I observed and assessed. Details of their language study and acquisition will follow. All of the non-native speakers learned ASL as adults. Native-like fluency takes a very long time and requires intense training to compensate for late exposure and learning. (Morford and Mayberry 2000)

The question that seems to naturally follow is: how difficult is it to learn ASL? The usual response is "about as difficult as it is to learn any foreign language." According to Jacobs (1996) one must consider its degree of foreignness. The Foreign Service Institute and the Defence Language Institute have grouped languages into four categories. Category 1 includes Spanish, French and German, for example. Each successive category requires more time in which to become proficient. The most difficult is Category 4. It includes languages such as Arabic, Chinese, Japanese and Korean. ASL is considered a Category 4 language. The time and aptitude it would take to learn a language in this category, for example, and be comfortably proficient using it, would be on average between six and fifteen years, based on 10 hours of language instruction per week. It is worth noting that a considerable number of the educational interpreters begin working in the classroom with fewer than three years of experience signing ASL. "While aptitude does not appear to play a significant role in first language acquisition, i.e., most people acquire their native language completely regardless of other cognitive abilities that they may possess, it has been implicated in L2 learning by adults. More importantly, aptitude should be a deciding

factor when accepting students into an interpreting program."
(Quinto-Pozos 2005)

My Observations

- Most of the educational interpreters interviewed reported they had never had a deaf teacher for their ASL classes.

- Many of them reported that they never had any formal ASL instruction.

- Many also reported that they never had any formal training for interpreting.

- Most were weak in their ability to accurately convey the actual meaning behind the words – they lacked semantic awareness in both ASL and English resulting in a skewing of the speaker's intent.

- Most of them learned ASL when they were an adult – which doesn't make fluency impossible, but they rarely interacted with deaf adults or children outside of work hours, which impeded their language progress. Many of the educational interpreters interviewed reported having very little contact with the Deaf community.

- Many of the requisite, co-occurring non-manual grammatical features were not realised or incorporated into their signed production. (Non-manual markers of grammatical constructions will be discussed in detail in the following section regarding skewing of a speaker's message.)

- Many interpreters were weak in their visual-spatial abilities. They had a very difficult time when they were required to go from a verbal text to "seeing" a visual representation of it in their mind's eye. Visual-spatial ability involves accurately perceiving an image, comprehending its properties, and then mentally modifying it, and producing a new image in a different form. (Gardner, 1991) For educational interpreters, the different 'form' would be ASL. The linguistic processing by speakers of English is very linear and sequential. The interpreters I observed struggled visibly in working from this linear format into to the three-dimensional and visual way of talking in ASL. It meant that they had to wait for the entire sentence to be uttered in order to understand and correctly align the objects in space. The classroom dynamics did not always allow the interpreters the luxury of this much processing time.

- Most of the interpreters were also very weak in their use of classifiers. Classifiers are an integral part of ASL. It is through the use of classifiers that ASL expresses such things as prepositions, location relationships, and plurality. It is also a means to provide adjectival information. "The use of classifiers consists of making a connection between the visual representation of reality in the mind and its linguistic expression. It is not uncommon that the level of mastery in classifiers is perceived as an indication of the degree of mastery in American Sign Language." (Kuntze in Lessard, 2002) It is not uncommon for second language learners of ASL to plateau in their L2 acquisition because they are not able to make much progress in comprehending and producing structures that incorporate classifiers. The three-dimensional properties of classifiers are unlike anything that speakers of English are accustomed to.

Bilingual Fluency

It has been said that interpreters need "superior linguistic skills and cultural knowledge to function successfully." (McIntire 1990) One of the most noticeable challenges to the interpreters I observed was the lack of training in the pragmatic use of language. When looking at "talk" or text atomically, one can miss the pragmatic influence; the way people intentionally craft their language and word choice, and fail to understand the overall thought or intention. The goal should be that the interpreted message be a true reflection of the speaker's intent, and not a literal, verbatim stream of meaningless words. "Experienced [interpreters] (5+ years) seemed to intuitively focus on the function of the discourse while paying attention to the meaning, whereas the less experienced interpreters chose words but didn't recognise the function or lacked strategies to show the function. Impact on students: higher level thinking processes not activated when interpretation lacks these processes." (Dr. Debra Russell, University of Alberta, Supporting Deaf People Conference, 2008)

What makes for a good interpretation? One measure of a successful interpretation is the amount of prosodic information that is included from the source language into the target language. Prosody is the combination of features in any language that produces the rhythm, accent and feel of the language (Winston 2000). Until recently, the function of prosody and its relation to discourse has been largely ignored in second language learning and teaching. In the literature on first language acquisition, however, the development of intonation and of prosody for discourse functions has been an important issue. The features of prosody in a spoken language include those that have linguistic relevance, as in the words themselves and the co-occurring intonation, accent, rhythm, pitch, stress, volume, tempo and speed. Features of prosody in ASL are carried by non-manual signals (NMS). (See Appendix A for a detailed listing of non manual signals in ASL.) In addition, and often overlooked or left out due to cognitive overload on the part of the interpreter, are the paralinguistic features that add meaning, but may not take on the form of a word, e.g., a sigh or moan.

In discourse, sentences need to be linked to other sentences in order to carry an idea through a series of changes in events and temporal contexts (Morgan 1999). One term used to define this technique is cohesion. Cohesion refers to relations that exist between sentences when the interpretation of some element in discourse is dependent on that of another (Halliday and Hasan 1976). This leads to the overall intelligibility of discourse. It is important that an interpreter knows the cohesion devices of both the source language and the target language and how to employ them correctly. An interpreter who is able to successfully incorporate the features of prosody will allow the deaf student to benefit from more native-like discourse.

Gile (1995) posits a set of three requirements for effective interpreting – linguistic knowledge, knowledge of the interpreting process and extralinguistic knowledge. Working at the discourse level requires the interpreter to discern extralinguistic features in the source language and express the equivalence in the target language.

Roda Roberts from the University of Ottawa, who has taught translation and interpreting in many Canadian, United States and Indian universities, is considered to be an authority on translation theory. She has published numerous articles and books on the training of translators and interpreters, terminology/lexicography, and community interpreting. She believes interpreters should be assessed on their ability to perform in the following three domains of competency. [italics mine]

Language Competency

1. The ability to work between two languages.
2. The ability to understand the source message **and all its nuances.**
3. The ability to express correctly the same message in the target language.

Transfer Competency

1. The ability to understand the meaning contained in the source message.
2. The ability to render the meaning of the source message into the target language **without distortions, additions or omissions.**
3. The ability to render the message from the source language into the target language without undue influence of the source language, i.e., vocabulary is in ASL, but the grammar is English.
4. The ability to render the message in **the same style or register.**

Subject Matter Competency

1. Since one cannot interpret what one cannot understand, knowledge of the subject or content is required in order to accurately convey the message.
2. Sufficient knowledge of the **specialised discourse** to interpret effectively.

Errors and Omissions Specific to Language and Transfer Competencies

- Omissions in terms of instructional content (unintelligible).
- Skewing of original message which, often intelligible, but did not have the same intent as the speaker's.
- Deletion of pronouns when they were needed for clarity.
- Pronoun copy (redundant use of at the end of a sentence)
- Omissions of critical cohesive devices – very difficult to follow

and parse the text; students said that it felt like one long sentence.
- Well-formed constructions of ASL Wh- and rhetorical questions – but pragmatically the wrong intent or discourse function (skewed), e.g. when the speaker was giving an imperative disguised as a question as in "Who left the door open?"
- Good sign production – but semantically the wrong sign choice, e.g. a woman who had suffered with multiple sclerosis and after several stays in the hospital "finally died" signed with the ASL PAH!, often glossed as finally, entailing success or accomplishment.
- Interpretation on the word level – unprocessed, literal utterances that usually conform to the grammar of English, not of ASL.
- Skewing on the pragmatic level – missing the more subtle use of language and discourse functions.

Discourse Competencies

When observing the classroom interpreters, a second type of error was noted – not because the interpreter was unfamiliar with the linguistics of ASL or English as delineated in the ASL fluency section, but because the context-specific use of language in which the discourse took place was not correctly realised. In conversation or classroom discourse, there is usually motivation behind what one says. ... [T]he meaning of the source text is inextricably tied to the context of a single communication event, and the interpreter must look to features of this surrounding circumstance for clues to the particular meaning intended by the words as they are used this one time. (Janzen, 2005) At the discourse level, interpreters need to listen to a full thought – which could be as long as a paragraph, in order to determine the intended meaning, which may or may not have been said explicitly. However, in the classroom, taking into consideration all the different parties involved and the classroom dynamics, the interpreter is rarely afforded the luxury of waiting that long before having to begin to sign.

In addition to the various types of discourse that took place in the classroom, the dynamics of all the parties involved at any given time were difficult for the interpreter to manage. It was not always the content of a lecture that was the challenge, rather the multiple channels of information that were present and active at the same time, e.g.:

- Classroom chatter before, during, after teacher lectures.
- Students interactions with other students.
- Announcements that were given over the loudspeaker or intercom.
- Classroom chatter before, during after the announcements.
- Other distractions such as environmental noises, e.g. lawnmowers, kids on the playground, construction on campus or nearby, etc – visual and auditory "noise" that distracted the other students as well as the interpreter and the deaf student.
- When the teacher showed a video which had an off screen narrator.
- When there were people on the screen who were also talking, sometimes simultaneously with the narrator, but perhaps at a lower volume.
- When the video image included an overlay of maps, diagrams or other graphics.
- The most challenging seemed to be the action scenes, which the students seemed to prefer watching, rather than witness the struggle of the interpreter attempting to describe or reconstruct what was happening.

In addition:

- Most of the interpreters were very weak in creating maps and other diagrams in their signing space.
- Many of the interpreted texts were confusing because the interpreter did not include a change in viewpoint when there needed to be one.
- When the interpreters went into a role shift (or constructed action) they did not align the elements of that part of the text with this new character's point of view.

Errors in Specific Constructions

A feature of ASL that is elusive to second language learners, easily overlooked, and yet instrumental for the role that it plays in ASL prosody and pragmatics is the set of non-manual signals that accompany the lexical items. It is important that an educational interpreter... "acquire both linguistic and affective facial expressions and ...distinguish their use in discourse." (Reilly et al 1990)

There is a construction in ASL that requires extensive use of non-manual signals and is one that I have found to be problematic for educational interpreters - conditional constructions. Conditionals are used to make inferences when the information is incomplete. It contributes to the development of a child's theory of mind. (See **Further Considerations** below). In addition, this construction allows one to think about alternative "hypothetical" situations, perhaps counter to what is currently seen in the world. "Understanding the conceptual and behavioural organisation of the ability to construct and interpret conditionals provides basic insight into the cognitive processes, linguistic competence and inferential strategies of human beings" (Traugott, etal p.3)

Conditional structures are a challenge to learners of ASL. They are complex in their syntactic structures; the non-manual signals of a conditional are much more elaborate than those showing affect; they can be expressed by a combination of a manual signal and a non-manual marker, or they can be shown by the non-manual markers without the sign.

Examples

Many of the interpreters observed did not listen to the full sentence before interpreting the sentences described below. As a result, there were notable errors that resulted in confusion on the part of the students.

The first example is a type of conditional that is called a condition hypothetical where an event or situation will happen provided that the condition is met. In English the condition is expressed using the word "if" but is just as often expressed using the words "as long as", or "with the understanding that"; and since many of the interpreters were working at the word level, the latter were where the errors occurred.

English sentence: I wouldn't mind teaching you how to drive *if* you'll wash my car.
A correct ASL equivalent: (topic) TO-DRIVE, ME TEACH-TO-YOU, DON'T MIND. *UNDERSTAND++,* (topic) MY CAR, YOU WASH IN-RETURN.
The ASL lexical item denoting the conditionality was UNDERSTAND++. I rarely observed this sign being used in conjunction with the correct non-manuals in the antecedent clause of the conditional.

The second example is one that *should* have been interpreted as a conditional (predictive) but because the sentence contained the word "when", the ASL wh-question sign (temporal) was used instead. A good test of a predictive conditional would be to replace the word 'when' with whenever. If the interpreter is working at the word level, or does not have ample time to process larger chunks of talk, i.e., being able to insert the word whenever to test for a conditional, the prediction will be missed and the message will be skewed.

English sentence: You have to wait; *when* the light comes on, it's ready.
An ASL equivalent: WAIT, *(brow raise to mark condition)*, LIGHT (become bright), READY

The third example is one that *should* have been interpreted as a conditional but the condition was implied. The English sentence did not contain the word "if". The interpreters gave it a literal translation.
English sentence: *[if you are wearing]* No shirt, *[and if you are wearing]* no shoes, *[then there will be]* no service
An ASL equivalent: *(Brow raise to mark conditional)*, NO SHIRT, NO SHOES, *(lower brow)*, NO SERVICE

The fourth was correctly interpreted as a Conditional (Cause and Effect). It contained the word "if", but because the first clause *absolutely* caused the second clause, the degree of conditionality was very strong and there should have been a transition sign, e.g., MEAN, used instead of THEN. The ASL sign MEAN is a transition sign used as an indication of the relationship between the first and clause. If the first clause *absolutely* causes the second, then MEAN is the transition word used. If the second clause *might* be caused by the first, then MAYBE is used. Very few educational interpreters used MEAN or MAYBE in their versions of this sentence. Most of them had not heard that there was a relationship factor associated with the words.

English sentence: I realised *if* the tree had fallen across the tracks, *[then]* the train would hit it and be derailed.

An ASL equivalent: I REALISE, SERIOUS DANGER, *(brow raise to mark condition)*, TREE FALL-ACROSS TRACK, TRAIN HIT TREE, FLY OFF TRACKS.

Further Considerations

Unfortunately the variables that need to be considered are greater than the length of this paper will allow.
Not included, but definitely worth exploring further is the effect of the interpreter on the cognitive development of the deaf child – in developing their intuitive understanding of the world and the ability to make inferences. It is through a strong Theory of Mind (ToM) that children are able to draw inferences. It is what allows them to make sense of what they encounter in the world, i.e., an understanding of cause and effect, and conditions. A child develops ToM gradually. Even older children have a difficult time understanding irony - why a person says one thing and means another; or why a question form was used with a non-question meaning, as in rhetorical questions.

What are the implications for deaf children who come from homes that don't share their language? And where they are not able to read either at the level or the speed of the captions at the movies or on TV? And where their family does not sit and share books with them? Or at school where the plot of a story is mediated through an interpreter who may not be fluent?

Because one cannot interpret what one does not understand, it is important that the educational interpreter have a strong academic background. While working with educational interpreters, I have seen far too frequently their lack of general world knowledge and limited English vocabulary. It is difficult to interpret information at educational levels beyond what one understands or has completed in one's own educational pursuits. Even worse is to have to interpret unfamiliar content. An education from a four- year institution affords the educational interpreter an exposure to content in a variety of courses. As a student in a BA program, one would have to write papers and demonstrate the ability to clearly express thoughts and ideas. It would also require a lot of reading and perhaps a course on public speaking. These qualities make for a well-rounded interpreter. Professional interpreters already working in the field in a variety of settings can attest to the value of a good education and its positive effect on their ability to interpret. To this end, at the 2003 RID Conference in Chicago, the membership passed a motion, which will eventually require a baccalaureate degree in order to stand for future performance interview tests. (See Appendix D for details).

Hopefully with the current requirements for educational interpreter qualifications being put forth in legislation, the evolution of the interpreter education programs to require both English and ASL language fluency as an entrance requirement, as a result to better prepare graduates to analyse ASL and English on a discourse level, and with more rigorous evaluation processes and a higher level of certification passing rates in place as a (minimum) standard for employment, we will find deaf students in the presence of the best people using the best processes (tools) to provide the best product (interpretation) with which to mediate their education.

References

Abe, I. (1980) How vocal pitch works. In C. van Schooneveld and L. Waugh (Eds.), *The melody of language: Intonation and prosody* (pp. 1-24). Baltimore, Maryland: University Park Press.

Anderson, D. & Reilly, J. S. (1998) Pah! The acquisition of adverbials in ASL. *Sign Language and Linguistics* Vol. 1, No. 2, 117-142.

Baker, C. (1977) Regulators and Turn-taking in American Sign Language discourse. In LA. Friedman (Ed.), *On the other hand: New perspectives on American Sign Language.* New York: Academic Press, Inc.

Baker, C. & Padden, C. (1978) Focusing on the nonmanual components of American Sign Language. In P. Siple (Ed.), *Understanding language through Sign Language research,* (pp 27-57), New York: Academic Press.

Bellugi, U. & Klima, E. (1990) Properties of visual spatial languages. In S. Prillwitz & T. Vollhaber (Eds.), Sign language research and application: proceedings of the international congress Hamburg March 23-25, 1990. Hamburg, Germany: Signum Press.

Bellugi, U., Mcintire, M, & Reilly, J. S. (1990) The acquisition of conditionals in American Sign Language: Grammaticized facial expression. *Applied Psycholinguistics, 11, 369-392.*

Bellugi, U. & Reilly, J. S. (1996) Competition on the face: affect and the language in ASL motherese. *Journal of Child Language* 23, 219-239.

Bonvillian, J.D., Orlansky, M.D., & Folven, R.J. (1994) Early Sign Language acquisition: implications for theories of language acquisition. In V. Volterra & C. Erting (Eds.), *From gesture to language in hearing and deaf children.* Washington, D.C.: Gallaudet University Press.

Coulter, G. (1978) RAISED EYEBROWS AND WRINKLED NOSES: The grammatical function of facial expression in relative clauses and related constructions. In F. Caccamise & D. Hicks (Eds.), *ASL in a bilingual, bicultural context proceedings of the second national symposium on Sign Language research and teaching* (pp. 65-74). Coronado, CA: NAD.

Davies, J. (2000) Translation Techniques in Interpreter education. In C. Roy (Ed.), *Innovative practices for teaching Sign Language interpreters.* Washington, D.C.: Gallaudet University Press.

Emmorey, K. (2002) *Language, cognition, and the brain: insights from Sign Language research.* New Jersey: Lawrence Erlbaum Associates.
Gardner, H. (1991) *The unschooled mind: how children think and how schools should teach.* (pp. 84-112). New York: Basicbooks.

Hatch, E. (1992) *Discourse and language education.* New York, NY: Cambridge University Press.

Hoiting, N., & Slobin, D. (2002) What a deaf child needs to see: advantages of a natural Sign Language over a sign system. In Schulmeister, R. and Reinitzer, H. (Eds.), *Progress in Sign Language research.* Hamburg, Germany: Signum-Verlag.

Jacobs, R. (1996) Just how hard is it to learn ASL? The case for ASL as a truly foreign language. In C. Lucas (Ed.), *Multicultural aspects of sociolinguistics in deaf communities.* Washington, D.C: Gallaudet University Press.

Larson, M. (1984) *Meaning-based translation: A guide to cross-language equivalence.* Lanham, MD: University Press of America, Inc.

LaBue, M.A. (1995). Language and learning in a deaf education classroom: Practice and paradox. In C. Lucas (Ed.), *Sociolinguistics in Deaf Communities,* Washington, D.C.: Gallaudet University.

Lieberman, P. (1980) The innate, central aspect of intonation. In C. van Schooneveld & L. Waugh (Eds.), *The melody of language: Intonation and prosody* (pp. 187-199). Baltimore, Maryland: University Park Press.

Marschark, M. (1997). *Raising and educating a deaf child.* New York: Oxford University Press.

Marschark, M., Sapere, P., Convertino, C., & Seewagen, R. (2005). Access to Postsecondary Education through Sign Language Interpreting. *Journal of Deaf Studies and Deaf Education, 10* (1).

Marschark, M., Sapere, P., Convertino, C., & Seewagen, R. (2005). Educational interpreting: Access and outcomes. In M. Marschark, R. Peterson & E. Winston (Eds.), Sign *Language Interpreting and Interpreter Education* (pp. 57-83). New York: Oxford University Press.

Mather, S. & Winston E. (1998) Spatial mapping and involvement in ASL storytelling. In C. Lucas (Ed.), *Pinky extension and eye gaze: Language use in deaf communities.* Washington, D.C.: Gallaudet University Press.

McIntire, M, (1990) The work and education of Sign Language interpreters. In S. Prillwitz & T. Vollhaber (Eds.), Sign language research and application: proceedings of the international congress Hamburg March 23-25, 1990. Hamburg, Germany: Signum Press.

Metzger, M. (1999) *Sign language interpreting: deconstructing the myth of neutrality.* Washington, D.C.: Gallaudet University Press.

Morford, J & Mayberry, R. (2000) A reexamination of "early exposure" and its implications for language acquisition by eye. In C. Chamberlain, J. Morford, & R. Mayberry (Eds.), *Language acquisition by eye.* Mahwah, New Jersey: Lawrence Erlbaum Associates.

Morgan, G. (1999) Event packaging in British Sign Language discourse. In E. Winston (Ed.), *Storytelling conversation discourse in deaf communities.* (pp. 59-82). Washington, D.C.: Gallaudet University Press.

Napier, J. (2003) A sociolinguistic analysis of the occurrence and types of omissions produced by Australian Sign language-English interpreters. In M. Metzger, S. Collins, V. Dively, & R. Shaw, (Eds.), *From topic boundaries to omission: new research on interpretation* (pp.99-145). Washington, D.C.: Gallaudet University Press.

Patschke, C.G. & Wilbur, R. (1998) Body leans and the marking of contrast in American Sign Language. *Journal of Pragmatics* 30, 275-303.

Pollitt, K., (2000) Critical linguistics and cultural awareness: essential tools in the interpreter's kit bag. In C. Roy (Ed.) *Innovative practices for teaching Sign Language interpreters.* Washington, D.C.: Gallaudet University Press.

Pratt, M.L & Traugott, E.C. (1980) *Linguistics for students in literature.* Orlando, Florida: Harcourt Brace Jovanovich, Inc.

Pyers, J. (2003) The expression of false belief in American Sign Language. In A Baker, B van den Bogaerde, & O. Crasborn (Eds.) Cross-*linguistic perspectives in Sign Language research: selected papers from TISLR 2000.* Hamburg, Germany: Signum Verlag.

Quinto-Pozos, D. (2005) Factors that influence the acquisition of ASL for interpreting students. In M. Marschark, R. Peterson, & E. Winston (Eds.) *Sign language interpreting interpreter education: directions for research and practice.* New York: Oxford University Press.

Ramsey, C.L. (1997). *Deaf children in public schools: Placement, context, and consequences.* Washington, DC: Gallaudet University Press.

Rayman, J. (1999) Storytelling in the visual mode: A comparison of ASL and English. In E. Winston (Ed.), *Storytelling conversation discourse in deaf communities.* (pp. 27-58). Washington, D.C.: Gallaudet University Press.

Reily, J., McIntire, M., & Bellugi, U. (1994) Faces: The relationship between language and affect. In V. Volterra & C. Erting (Eds.) *From gesture to language in hearing and deaf children.* Washington, D.C.: Gallaudet University Press.

Roy, C.B. (1989) Feature of discourse in an American Sign Language lecture. In C. Lucas (Ed.) *The Sociolinguistics of the Deaf Community*. New York: Academic Press.

Roy, C.B. (2000) Training interpreters-past, present, and future. In C. Roy (Ed) *Innovative practices for teaching Sign Language interpreters*. Washington, D.C.: Gallaudet University Press.

Schick, B. & Williams, K. (1998). Profile of skills at each rating level if the EIPA. http://www.boystownhospital.org/EIPA/index.asp.

Schick, B., Williams, K. & Bolster, L. 1999. Skill levels of educational interpreters working in public schools. *Journal of Deaf Studies and Deaf Education, 4* (2), 144-155.

Schick, B., Williams, K., & Kupermintz, H. (2006). Look who's being left behind: Educational interpreters and access to education for deaf and hard-of-hearing students. *Journal of Deaf Studies and Deaf Education 11*, 3-20.

Schick, B. A model of learning within an interpreted K-12 educational setting. Supporting Deaf People Conference, 2008.

Schley, S. (1996) What's a clock? "Suppose the alarm lights are flashing...?: Sociolinguistic and educational implications of comparing ASL and English word definitions. In C. Lucas (Ed) *Multicultural aspects of sociolinguistics in deaf communities. Washington*, D.C : Gallaudet University Press.

Selkirk, E.O. (1995) Sentence prosody: Intonation, stress, and phrasing. In J. Goldsmith (Ed.), *The hand book of phonological theory* (pp.550-569). Cambridge, MA: Blackwell.

Snow, C.E. (1999) Social perspectives on the emergence of language. In B. MacWhinney (Ed) *The emergence of language.* (pp 257-273). Mahwah, New Jersey

Stewart, D.A., & Kluwin, T.N. 1999. The gap between guidelines, practices, and knowledge in interpreting services for deaf students. *Journal of Deaf Studies and Deaf Education, 1*, 29-39.

Volterra, V. (1990) Sign language acquisition and bilingualism. In S. Prillwitz & T. Vollhaber (Eds) *Sign language research and application:*

proceedings of the international congress Hamburg March 23-25, 1990. Hamburg, Germany: Signum Press.

Wilbur, R.B. (1997) A prosodic/pragmatic explanation for word order variation in ASL with typological implications. In K. Lee, E. Sweetser, & M. Verspoor (Eds.), *Lexical and syntactic constructions and the construction of meaning* (pp. 89-104). Philadelphia: John Benjamims.

Wilbur, R.B. (2000) Phonological and prosodic layering of non-manuals in American Sign Language. Festschrift for Klima & Bellugi.

Winston, B. (2000) It doesn't look like ASL! Defining, recognizing, and teaching prosody in ASL. *Proceedings of the 13th National Convention, Conference of Interpreter Trainers: "CIT at 21: Celebrating excellence, celebrating partnership."* Maryland: Registry of Interpreters for the Deaf, Inc.

Winston, E.A. (1994). An interpreted education: Inclusion or exclusion. In R.C. Johnson, & O.P.Cohen (Eds.), *Implications and complications for deaf students of the full inclusion movement.* Gallaudet Research Institute Occasional Paper 94-2. Washington, DC: Gallaudet University.

Yule, G. (1985) *The study of language* (second edition). New York, NY: Cambridge University Press.

Appendix A: Non Manual Signals

Brow raise

An ASL phrase that contains raised eyebrows used grammatically and not for affect, is there to describe the background information. It provides the "scene" from which the second clause can be interpreted. This is true for the antecedent clause in a conditional. The raised eyebrows co-occur with each sign in this clause. If the subsequent clause is a yes-no question, the brows do not get lowered as they normally would.

Body lean

A forward lean can mark that a certain interaction is taking place with the addressee. Perhaps the speaker is expecting a response of some kind. This is true for a yes-no question that contains a forward lean. A forward lean is also present in a rhetorical yes-no question, even though the speaker is not expecting an answer from the listener. Rhetorical constructions will be discussed in a later section.

Eye blink

Eye blinks are present in conditionals to mark the boundaries between the two clauses. According to Baker and Cokely (1980) this occurs at the juncture between the conditional and the following clause along with other non-manual activity, namely a pause, the lowering of the eyebrows and a shift in the head or body orientation.

Head rotation

Head rotation refers to the rotating movement of the signer's head either to the left or to the right. It is similar to the way the head moves in a rhetorical question. Head rotation to a greater or lesser degree was consistently noticed in conditional sentences. (Liddell 1986) The scope of the head rotation is the antecedent clause. It will not occur when there is the side-to-side movement of the head as in a negative headshake.

Head thrust

This is a term that Liddell coined in 1986 to mean the single outward and downward movement of the head. This non-manual was consistently present in his corpus of ASL conditionals. Even though the head rotation is maintained throughout the antecedent, the head thrust is only present during the final sign of the clause. He also noted that there were when-clauses in his data that had evidence of a raised brow and head-thrust. "When" has also been recognised as a marker of a conditional for spoken languages. During a class lecture, for example, the teacher might say, "When the solution turns yellow, it indicates the presence of carbon dioxide." I have observed educational interpreters using the citation form of the sign WHEN, which represents a wh-question, e.g., "When will we get there?" instead of the correct non-manual marker for conditionality.

Eye gaze

A change in the direction of the eye gaze is present in some conditional constructions. It is an indication of a new role or character being created in the discourse. As a result of the change in eye gaze (point-of-view or perspective), there is a newly constructed space in which this new character will reside. The narrator moves in and out of this space when performing a particular type of conditional.

Appendix B: State required minimal EIPA standards

- New Jersey, Kansas, Kentucky, Louisiana, North Carolina and Wisconsin – 3.0
- Arizona, Colorado, Indiana, Maine, Nebraska, and Utah – 3.5
- California and Nevada – 4.0

Interpreters require a great deal of training in order to meet minimum standards. Unfortunately, educational interpreting is an emerging profession and educators are only now beginning to understand the range of skills that are necessary to do the job well. Minimum qualifications of an educational interpreter should include:

- A formal assessment of interpreting skills

- - An Educational Interpreter Performance Assessment (EIPA) score of at least a 4.0
  - Registry of Interpreters for the Deaf (RID) certification
  - NAD-RID certification (NIC) at a certified level
  - NAD certification of at least a 4.0
- Degree or coursework in an educationally-related field
  - BA degree (preferred)
  - Graduate of an Interpreter Training Program
- 24 – 30 credit hours of educational coursework
- A formal assessment of content knowledge related to educational interpreting (for example, a passing score on the EIPA Written Test)
- The ability to perform as a professional member of the educational team (For example, as stated in the Educational Interpreter Performance Assessment Code of Professional Conduct).

Research shows that even graduates of two-year Interpreter Training Programs may not meet a common standard held in many states – an EIPA rating of 3.5.

Unqualified interpreters cannot provide access to Free and Appropriate Public Education (FAPE). Research shows that interpreters who fall below minimum standards omit and distort much of teacher and peer communication. When an interpreter is not highly qualified, a deaf or hard of hearing student misses vital classroom communication and does not receive adequate access to the general education curriculum.

EIPA Rating System

The evaluation team uses an EIPA rating form to evaluate the interpreter's abilities. The samples are rated in the following domains:

1. Grammatical skills: use of prosody (or intonation), grammar, and space.
2. Sign-to-voice interpreting skills: ability to understand and convey child/teen Sign Language

3. Vocabulary: ability to use a wide range of vocabulary, accurate use of fingerspelling and numbers
4. Overall abilities: ability to represent a sense of the entire message, use appropriate discourse structures, and represent who is speaking.

Evaluators use a Likert Scale to assess specific skills. Scores for each skill range from 0 (no skills demonstrated) to 5 (advanced native-like skills). The scores from all three evaluators are averaged for each skill area, each domain, as well as the overall test score. An individual's EIPA score is the summary total score. For example, an interpreter should report her score as EIPA Secondary PSE 4.2, which shows which grade level, which language, and the total summary EIPA score.

Descriptions of each EIPA Level

Level 1: Beginner

Demonstrates very limited sign vocabulary with frequent errors in production. At times, production may be incomprehensible. Grammatical structure tends to be nonexistent. Individual is only able to communicate very simple ideas and demonstrates great difficulty comprehending signed communication. Sign production lacks prosody and use of space for the vast majority of the interpreted message.

An individual at this level is not recommended for classroom interpreting.

Level 2: Advanced Beginner

Demonstrates only basic sign vocabulary and these limitations interfere with communication. Lack of fluency and sign production errors are typical and often interfere with communication. The interpreter often hesitates in signing, as if searching for vocabulary. Frequent errors in grammar are apparent, although basic signed sentences appear intact. More complex grammatical structures are typically difficult. Individual is able to read signs at the word level and simple sentence level but complete or complex sentences often require repetitions and repairs. Some use of prosody and space, but use is inconsistent and often incorrect.

An individual at this level is not recommended for classroom interpreting.

Level 3: Intermediate

Demonstrates knowledge of basic vocabulary, but will lack vocabulary for more technical, complex, or academic topics. Individual is able to sign in a fairly fluent manner using some consistent prosody, but pacing is still slow with infrequent pauses for vocabulary or complex structures. Sign production may show some errors but generally will not interfere with communication. Grammatical production may still be incorrect, especially for complex structures, but is in general, intact for routine and simple language. Comprehends signed messages but may need repetition and assistance. Voiced translation often lacks depth and subtleties of the original message. An individual at this level would be able to communicate very basic classroom content, but may incorrectly interpret complex information resulting in a message that is not always clear.

An interpreter at this level needs continued supervision and should be required to participate in continuing education in interpreting.

Level 4: Advanced Intermediate

Demonstrates broad use of vocabulary with sign production that is generally correct. Demonstrates good strategies for conveying information when a specific sign is not in their vocabulary. Grammatical constructions are generally clear and consistent, but complex information may still pose occasional problems. Prosody is good, with appropriate facial expression most of the time. May still have difficulty with the use of facial expression in complex sentences and adverbial non-manual markers. Fluency may deteriorate when rate or complexity of communication increases. Uses space consistently most of the time, but complex constructions or extended use of discourse cohesion may still pose problems. Comprehension of most signed messages at a normal rate is good but translation may lack some complexity of the original message.

An individual at this level would be able to convey much of the classroom content but may have difficulty with complex topics or rapid turn-taking.

Level 5: Advanced

Demonstrates broad and fluent use of vocabulary, with a broad range of strategies for communicating new words and concepts. Sign production errors are minimal and never interfere with comprehension. Prosody is correct for grammatical, non-manual markers, and affective purposes. Complex grammatical constructions are typically not a problem. Comprehension of sign messages is very good, communicating all details of the original message.

An individual at this level is capable of clearly and accurately conveying the majority of interactions within the classroom.

Appendix C: CI and CT (Generalist) Rating Scales

RID has recently implemented a new rating system for the Certificates of Interpretation and Transliteration performance tests. This system is based on a set of 13 items, which we refer to as behaviourally anchored scales. These items represent key behaviours an interpreter must demonstrate in order to be awarded certification. The 13 behaviours are scored on a 1-5 Likert-type scale, with one being low and five being high. They are weighted according to criticality and importance to the task in order to correspond to the St. Paul standard voted on by the certified membership in 1987. There are seven scales/behaviours for the voice-to-sign (V-S) section, and six for the sign-to-voice (S-V) section. These 13 scales (items) are duplicated for the one-to-one section of the test as the candidate does both V-S and S-V. Therefore a candidate for certification is rated on 26 scales. There are three categories of raters: Deaf consumers, hearing consumers, and certified interpreters. A candidate's tape of their performance is sent to a rater in each of the three categories.

A general description of the seven scales for the Voice-to-Sign segment are:

1) Sign parameters - correct and consistent production of sign parameters (handshape, palm orientation, location and movement).

2) Flow - comfort level of sign flow; example - smooth, comfortable for viewing, not choppy with few false starts and unnecessary pauses, not over smooth without appropriate pauses.

3) Message equivalence - message completion with regard to factual information, register and cultural/linguistic adjustments with few minor miscues (omissions/substitutions, additions, and intrusions).

4) Target language - uses appropriate target language (e.g. signed English for the transliteration test and ASL for the interpretation test).

5) Affect - consistency of facial grammar and affect to source language.

6) Vocabulary choice - conceptually correct sign choices based on meaning rather than form.

7) Sentence boundaries - clear and consistent identification of sentence types and topic boundaries which match source language.

A general description of the six scales for the sign-to-voice segment of the test are:

8) Enunciation - clarity and consistency throughout task.

9) Flow - comfort level for listening; example: few false starts, pauses, and non-linguistic behaviours (distracting mannerisms - uh, um, etc.), not over smooth without appropriate pauses.

10) Message equivalence - message completion with regard to factual information, register and cultural/linguistic adjustments with few minor miscues (omissions/substitutions, additions, and intrusions).

11) Inflection - consistency of inflection to source language.

12) Vocabulary choice - conceptually correct sign choices based on meaning rather than form.

13) Sentence boundaries - clear and consistent identification of sentence types and topic boundaries which match source language.

Appendix D: RID Certification Requirements

Degrees necessary beginning in 2008 for performance testing applicants

At the 2003 RID Conference in Chicago, the membership passed a motion, which requires a degree in order to stand for future performance interview tests. It is important to note that these requirements are not immediate. In 2008, applicants who are hearing will be required to have a minimum of an associate's degree in order to be considered a candidate for certification. This means that they can take written or knowledge tests without a degree, but must have the degree in order to apply for the interview and performance sections of any test.

In 2012, applicants who are hearing will be required to have a minimum of a bachelor's degree in order to be considered a candidate for certification while applicants who are deaf will be required to have a minimum of an associate's degree.

In 2016, applicants who are deaf will be required to have a minimum of a bachelor's degree.

Additionally, there will be exceptions to the requirement. Those exceptions will be formulated and publicised no later than 2006.

The following is the text of the motion as approved at conference:

C 2003.05

- *RID adopt and publicise the following schedule for when all test candidates must have a degree from an accredited institution to stand for any RID certificate:*
- *Effective June 30, 2008, candidates for RID certification must have a minimum of an associate's degree. Effective June 30, 2012, Deaf candidates must have a minimum of an associate's degree.*
- *Effective June 30, 2012, candidates for RID certification must have a minimum of a bachelor's degree. Effective June 30, 2016, Deaf candidates must have a minimum of a bachelor's degree.*
- *By June 30, 2006, the Certification Council shall establish equivalent alternative criteria allowable in lieu of the educational requirements such as one or more of the following:*
- *Life experience, years of professional experience, years of education (credit hours) not totaling a formal degree.*

National Council on Interpreting (In response to motion L from the 2001 conference.)

Summary of the conference discussion

The discussion began with more clarification on the EIPA. It is administered nationally. Now it is the only test accepted by RID for educational interpreting certification. More than 25 states require the EIPA. State level requirements are more than a collective agreement. State-level departments of education have legal jurisdiction over kindergarten through high school education. They typically develop rules (although the name can differ across states). These rules have the legal effect of law. There is no national organisation, including teachers' professional organisations, who trump the state departments' of education rights to establish rules and practices. The U.S. federal government has issued statements that establishing legal requirements and responsibility's for educational interpreters remains the right of the states.

Change must come at a state level and must involve educators. Interpreters cannot impose changes or rules, even national organisations. Understanding how educational practices are defined is essential to affecting change. It is actually one of the reasons the EIPA is so widely recognised in educational settings. In addition to being a psychometrically valid test, those who devised the EIPA worked extensively with states to provide them with data about why requirements are essential and how to set up a statewide system to do this. While certification does not guarantee flawless work, it at least identifies a minimum level competencies.

Research has elicited data on about 140 RID-certified interpreters who have taken the EIPA. The average score is 4.2 on the EIPA. Often people talk about educational interpreters as being under-qualified (which many are). However, errors can be found in any interpretation. A recent study looked at the content conveyed by educational interpreters as well as 3 RID-certified interpreters. The RID-certified interpreters all had deaf family members, they had more than 25 years of experience, and were identified by the Deaf community as being "top" interpreters. However, on analysis of their interpretation, two of these experienced interpreters conveyed only 75% of the information correctly (from a 4th grade art lesson). Both conveyed about 50% of the Theory of Mind talk produced by the teacher. In fact, the RID-certified interpreter who made almost as many errors as the educational interpreters finished the testing by saying - "that was easy". She seemed unaware of her own performance.

We should not see interpreting errors as simply the result of an interpreter's "skill". The RID-certified interpreters were very skilled. However, like all interpreters, they were making decisions about what was important to convey and they were working within the constraints of the teacher's talk. The situation causes the 25% loss – i.e. lack of preparation, lack of understanding of the teacher's goals, etc.

It therefore is unfair to identify specifically errors produced by educational interpreters given that all interpreters make these errors. There are interpreters working in the adult community who are not qualified as well. But educational interpreters get singled out as being uniquely "unqualified".

Data also shows that interpreters who graduate from interpreter training programmes (ITPs) are only slightly more qualified than those who did not. ITPs routinely advise their graduates to work in the educational setting until they gain skills to work in the community. ITPs need to produce interpreters who are qualified to work and they need to stop using schools as their training grounds. Telling graduates to go practise on children seems profoundly unethical.

However, interpreters come out of training programmes and they have to start somewhere. Hopefully they will start work in a supportive environment where they can shadow and work in settings supported by more experienced interpreters. Hopefully they will be mentored and supervised and their workload guided to ensure that they are suitable for the assignments they undertake. Sadly this isn't always the case, and many start out immediately working on a freelance basis. Although this is undesireable, in some situations this is inevitable. Even when supervised every interpreter has to start working alone at some point in their career. And where should this be? Is it the college lecture, or the job interview or the doctors appointment or a high profile launch of some governmental project? None of them is straightforward and, with the probable exception of the latter, all can be potentially life determining in some form or another.

It may be impossible to alter the fact that newly trained interpreters will work in educational settings. What we really need to do is ensure that their training prepares them for this type of work more specifically than it does at present.

One delegate shared the following:

> "I must admit that I advise my students that if they are going to start in education, they should start in adult education like a community college - one where the consumer hopefully has basic literacy skills and the demands could be less challenging. I tell them to start with classes that they have either taken already or subjects they are very familiar with so the content of the course will not be a demand. I also remind them that it will be working with adults who have hopefully gotten past all the quirks that show up in middle school and high school - hormones, relationships, etc. I also tell them that they will have a better chance of working with a team if they start at a college. Many of the colleges here have placement tests so the interpreter can begin in classes that are less 'lecture driven' (though often classifier-rich as in Art and PE)."

At some point a field defines the qualifications that are minimal standards for entry. They are never enough in most professions. We need to advocate for interpreter coordinators in schools who can monitor, mentor, train, set standards, etc. Our school model needs to acknowledge that newly minted interpreters still need support, much like teachers. There is shared responsibility for training and continued support for fledgling interpreters out there.

One delegate felt that the grammatical features of ASL (particularly non-manual markers) are the least understood by interpreters. But this problem is shared by many interpreters working in all settings. A lack of ASL features is often misunderstood to be signed English. An interpreter lacking these features is not 'more English' but rather is lacking important features of Sign Language, whatever variety we might be calling it. Some interpreters keep their eyebrows raised continuously, or raise and lower them seemingly arbitrarily. This can be very confusing although Deaf people are often good at figuring out what poor signers are trying to say.

Another point which was raised was about pairing disfluency with disfluency. Some interpreters and administrators seem to think it is appropriate to place a deaf student who doesn't sign very well (all too common) with an interpreter who doesn't sign well in ASL. What someone means by this kind of comment is open to interpretation, but it should be stressed that non-manual ASL features give the signed message a grammaticality and a clarity that will make the message much more comprehensible to a signer of whatever variety of signed language they use. Deaf people who have less than native fluency can nearly always understand more sign than they can produce. It used to be the case that many training programmes advised interpreters to 'match' a deaf person's language, which if applied in the way described above is not good practice. It would appear that this is precisely the situation in which we find untrained interpreters and non-native signing deaf children in the school systems. More reason, perhaps, to fight against the use of sign systems, rather than ASL, in schools.

Practical Application of the Demand Control Schema with an Educational Interpreter: A Case Study by Kendra Keller

Introduction

Dean and Pollard (2001) adapted the Demand-Control[1] concept from research conducted by Robert Karasek (1979) and Törres Theorell (Karasek & Theorell, 1990). For more information about the D-C concept, see http://www.urmc.rochester.edu/dwc/edu/Control_Schema.htm

This paper examines the application of the Demand-Control schema for supervision and mentoring of interpreters.

In 1:1 supervision, an interpreter recounts the situation she chooses to assess, learns to recognise and evaluate the Demands, the work requirements or factors which call for a response; the Controls, decisions made in addressing them, (resources and strategies employed in response), as well as potential alternate controls. The interpreter's narrative about one situation is then re-conceptualised and structured into many of the Demand Control Schema (DC-S) elements.

The interpreter considers the effect, or positive and negative consequences, of her choices and any need for follow-through if resulting demands occur.

By learning and employing the schema, the interpreter becomes conscious of her work on a product level. Awareness of the demands increases, as does subsequent responsiveness.

---

[1] For more information see "Demand Control Schema" Deaf Wellness Center
http://www.urmc.rochester.edu/dwc/edu/Control_Schema.htm

In the recounting of events during the assignment, both the process and construct of the DC-S, as well as its ethical focus, provide for validation (feedback that what she is feeling, noticing and responding to makes sense according to the situation and fits into the structure of the DC-S) as well as the opportunity to consider alternate or new control options.

The interpreter is also engaged in a process to develop critical thinking skills, practice ethical decision-making, and identify further resources for successful and ethical decision making in the future.

Demand? Control? Consequence? EIPI? Qué es esto?

Use of the Demand Control Schema "will provide a framework for understanding the range of variables that are relevant to interpreting work. It will offer tools to identify which variables are most salient in a given assignment and how best to respond, *especially when the prevailing variables are not linguistic or cultural ones*.*" - Dean, R.K. And Pollard, R.Q., "...*It All Depends" Deaf Wellness Center http://www.urmc.rochester.edu/dwc/edu/Workshops.htm*
(*author's emphasis)

While not an explanation of the Demand Control Schema, this paper does offer one practical application of the DC-S, supporting its use in response to these critical questions:

What is available to assess what the work truly requires, for each of us - interpreting program graduates as they enter the (often solo) working world, working interpreters (Deaf and hearing) who may not have been trained in the DC-S, and the rapidly expanding community of mentors?

1. In a pragmatic and applied sense.
2. To consider the people we work with - deaf and hearing - and each other.
3. In each setting - in the context of specific environments, interactions, with particular vocabulary, with awareness of the goals for communication of everyone involved.

4. To help understand the "rules of interaction" (explicit and implied).
5. To gauge the impact of an interpreter's own internal process as it supports or detracts from the work.
6. To develop meta-cognition and recognition of decisions and resources.
7. To create an awareness of the power and myriad decisions we are making or could make.
8. To provide an ongoing, dynamic means to assess the many variables and outcomes in each situation, as well as a productive dialogue of such.

Learning, practicing and applying the Demand Control Schema (DC-S) provides an interpreter with tools to continue to meet the challenges of interpreting. It becomes a "lens through which"[1] we can become conscious of and able to express why and how our ethical decisions are made and take responsibility for their outcome. It provides a supportive process and measure of consequence, effect, responsiveness and responsibility. Even the most mundane of interpreting jobs, when studied via a framework providing a compassionate eye, provides great learning, validation, creativity and respect for an ethical practice.

When used correctly, the DC-S provides this framework. There is great value fairly quickly from simply acknowledging the demands as well as from the process of unpacking the package that we deliver. When used with guides who are experienced working with the DC-S, the process is innately validating and illuminating. The DC-S process is sustainable independently as well as in consultation with each other, in supervision, in interpreting program curriculae and on a systemic level. Its applications are only beginning to be discovered and developed. The creators of the DC-S are responsive and readily available to those undertaking this work. Access to resources, support and receptivity to new ways of applying the schema are encouraged.

---

[1] personal communication with Smith, A., 2008

The Demand Control Schema is most effectively used with ample time to practice its application. This paper will merely illustrate a few points that were captured in dialogue and thought to be of value. They are offered in the spirit of demystifying a valuable technique in furthering the integrity of our work.

The Process

A pre-certified interpreter, studying for certification, had been participating in a study group aimed at helping the members prepare for certification (NIC and/or the EIPA). Concurrent one-to-one consultations provided for more intensive work as the time to take the exam neared, specifically to prepare for the ethical portion of the exam. The pre-certified interpreter had studied the DC-S in her interpreting program but had not had much practice in applying it in this first year of work as an educational interpreter. The mentor began to use the DC-S, which served to refine and focus previous efforts and ideas for guiding protégés through a process of preparation for certification and ongoing supervision.

The interpreter provided a video sample of a fairly typical day in a high school classroom in which she regularly interpreted. The video sample was used for many levels of discussion, including language and interpreting process analysis and re-working, self-assessment of the actual interpretation, and discussion of ethical and other challenges the setting presented.

This presentation is based on notes from the 1:1 meetings, review of the video, as well as a later conversation which was videotaped, after the mentor had further training in using the DC-S, to follow up on the video sample and any ethical dilemmas that the pre-certified interpreter felt were unresolved.

The Setting

Public High School (grades 9-12), predominantly hearing students and teachers. This school serves as a "feeder school" meaning students are channelled into this school from a nearby elementary school with deaf students, and upon graduation from this high school, students tend to be channelled into local community colleges and quite frequently have the same interpreters in college. There were approximately 40 deaf and hard of hearing students in both mainstreamed and self-contained classrooms. Staff and faculty in the program at this school included one deaf teacher, one deaf aide, who worked in the self-contained classroom[1], 14 Interpreters, 2 with certification (one has deaf parents), 5 pre-certified [2] all from interpreter education programs, 7 non-certified (one from an interpreter education program).

The setting is in a physical science class. The topic of the lecture and activity is natural selection. This class period consisted primarily of an activity based on prior lectures and readings. Class began with the teacher explaining that the activity required students to go to several different "stations" located throughout the room, and complete different "challenges" at each station. She moved throughout the room as she talked. Some of the activities were to be timed. All were designed to mimic genotype and phenotype characteristics for determination of survival, for example, one's speed in figuring out a maze, physical attributes such as height to reach "fruit" in a tree or a person's size to fit into a "cave" for protection. Students were to work in teams, collect and record data on their experience. The two deaf students paired with each other.

---

[1] Self-contained Classroom: A day program for deaf students, who are segregated from the rest of the student population or perhaps mainstreamed into a few but not all classes during the day.
[2] Pre-certified: interpreters who have passed the written exam for certification and have a goal of certification

Stations

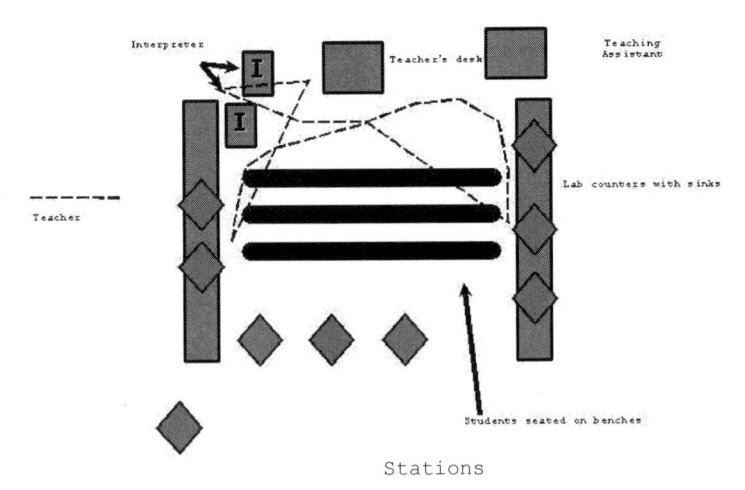

Class composition was a combination of sophomores, juniors, seniors (students in their second, third and fourth years of high school. The total number of students in class on this day was 30-40, mostly Caucasian, with many (assumed by the interpreter to be) Latino and Asian.

This class was taking place during the middle of the semester. Class period was 1 hour and 35 minutes, without a break. Staff and faculty in the classroom included one teacher, and two interpreters, and one teacher's aide, grading papers at a desk at the front of the room, not participating with the class.

There are two deaf students, both female, one using American Sign Language and one who uses Signing Exact English (SEE Sign), speech reads and speaks. One student is Filipina and the other Caucasian. The student who uses ASL is a senior (in her final year of high school), The SEE Signing student is a sophomore (in her second year of high school) who "grew up with SEE sign".

The interpreter who participated in this dialogue graduated from an interpreter education program in the spring of 2005 and identifies as a Caucasian, hearing female, in her first year of interpreting. Two interpreters are teamed. The team interpreter has some formal training, uses primarily SEE sign and is not certified. She was described as being of East Asian and Caucasian ethnicity, female. The two interpreters have experience teaming with each other and "work well together". They are of a similar age range, 20-30 years old. These traits are controls. Ethnicity, Age, Gender: all impact human communication when combined with the dynamics of the situation and so are listed although not specifically analyzed.

The interpreters learned what the topic and activity for the class would be just as class was starting. In other words, there is no "preparation time before class". This is a demand/control interaction if there is time and it is not taken advantage of, or if the school is not making allowances for prep time.

In her non-structured narrative, the interpreter identified the following factors. While she recounted, the mentor restructured them in writing, using the DC-S. A few examples of the restructured demands and controls are given. The purpose is to provide insight into the natural process and not an in-depth analysis. Video samples of the interpreter's work within the classroom, the post discussion from which these examples were taken, and the interpreter's own insights were shown during the presentation format.

The Narrative

"The classroom is noisy, the teacher is talking really fast. The teacher interrupts her explanation to the students to respond to questions, to reprimand students, who are talking, shouting, walking on desks, and to respond to requests to use the bathroom, go to the office, etc. It is chaotic."

Judgment language - restructuring the case presentation to remove language that contains qualitative judgments or is evaluative ("tense", "chaotic", "exciting", etc.) helps with lessening an interpretation of the demands based on our own filters and issues. It may be more difficult for others to understand what we mean when we use evaluative language. It is more effective, therefore, to state what happened in a neutral fashion when we communicate with each other to avoid automatically responding as if a judgment is accurate. As interpreters, we may respond to our own judgments rather than to the actual demand/control interaction. It can be more challenging to identify our own intrapersonal demands within the interpersonal demand category. In the presentation, this was discussed as part of the Thought Worlds of participants and so is clarified here.

Example of restructuring:

- The students are talking to each other while the teacher is talking
- The students are walking around
- The students are getting up on the desks
- The students are interrupting the teacher while she is presenting information
- The teacher is walking about to different parts of the classroom while she is talking
- The teacher's radio on her desk is turned on and music is playing

The interpreter states the following challenge: "Each station contains concepts embedded within concepts." Mentor asks, "For example?"

One station contains a paper plate that symbolises a leaf on the ground. There is water in the plate, symbolic of rainwater that has collected in the curled leaf. The task is to see how much water you can drink out of the leaf without using your hands. For the station asking "How far can you jump?" the teacher asked this question: "if a saber-toothed tiger was chasing you, you came to the edge of a cliff and you wanted to jump across to the other side, with no running start, how far can you jump?" Height - does your height allow you to reach the "fruit" on a tree? Bitterness - does the ability to taste the chemical on PTC paper (a chemically treated paper which some people have the gene to taste and some do not) help you avoid "poison berries"?

The interpreter goes on to explain the situation, "It's my first year interpreting", the video camera is recording her work (the demand being her desire to show good work product), and, she says, she has "an attitude about this class" because it is so hard (for which she is employing a control option to maintain a "transparent interpreting process" - examples of specifically how she does this are provided later).

The interpreter reported feeling like she wanted someone (like the head teacher or academic counselors) to come in and evaluate whether or not the interpretation was "working," (a response to the demand/control interactions which caused the complexity of the task). She may have been asking for an alternate control, or, someone to monitor interpretation effectiveness. For example, "They asked the interpreters to teach Sign Language to the deaf students." (Demand). "I told them no - get a deaf person." Control – she encouraged the school's quest to provide language support to the deaf students and interpreters by suggesting a native signer be brought in to model and teach Sign Language. Note: instruction in ASL was provided only to the deaf students in the self-contained classroom.

The interpreter continues, "When I look to my team interpreter she doesn't have the information I missed. My team interpreter looks at me for vocabulary. I give her the signs she needs." (This could be a demand/control interaction for which there are insufficient controls – lack of necessary sign vocabulary, still-developing processing speed, competing demands of the environmental noise and information being presented, etc.).

When the deaf students were looking over at the station during the verbal explanation of a physical setup, physical activity, visual information/attention was required as part of the explanation, and physical movements were being described, so the challenge was "knowing when to hold back and ... being a new interpreter... using all my brain power to get the message out there" and the subsequent increase in anxiety.

Rephrased: When the teacher explains each station, the deaf students look over to that station and away from the interpreter (demand). The teacher is unaware of this (demand). The interpreters are seated at the front of the classroom (control), and the stations are located throughout the room (demand). Additionally, when there is commotion, the deaf students look over to see what happened. There are competing visual demands on deaf students (demand). The interpreter is not standing next to the teacher as she moves to each station (this is a control). The interpreter is attempting to retain information the teacher is saying until the students look back to her (demand/control interaction). The difficulty in retaining the information could be a resulting demand based on the demand/control interaction between her skills and the dense information, or a negative consequence – dense information and her controls may be insufficient to respond (and maybe no one could).

The interpreter is in her first year of interpreting post graduation (this is a control). She is currently using auditory memory more than visual memory and knows it is a developmental phase in her skills, making it difficult to retain all the information.

She continues: "The deaf students give responsibility for vocabulary choices to the interpreters." The mentor asks "What happened?" The interpreter asks students their sign for "Natural Selection" and the student (signs the sign FLICK SHOULDER (points) IX - interpreter) 'not my responsibility', "You (interpreter) decide." This is a resulting demand. The interpreter suggests the signs "NATURE (NORMAL/NATIVE) and CHOOSE" for natural selection. This is a new control. The students agree with the signs.

Another challenge – "the deaf students do not take the initiative to interrupt if they miss something or do not understand," and "the teacher is 'awkward' with the deaf students and relies on the interpreters to take full responsibility for the deaf students' needs, including questions." Demands?
The mentor's question - "What happens, what did you see?" "When the deaf student raised her hand, the teacher stopped her lecture abruptly and asked 'is everything okay!?' All the other students in the class look over to the interpreters/deaf students. The deaf student's question is voiced and the teacher responds to the interpreter with 'tell her that...'" Subsequently, the student asks the interpreter her question rather than the teacher. The interpreter prompts the student to ask the teacher, and, the student declines.

The interpreter is also responding to what is identified here as a constellation of demands, the fact that the deaf students use two different modes of communication, present concurrent demands. She says, "what do I do with that? Try to shoot somewhere in the middle?" The restatement is:

The deaf student who uses SEE Sign is actively listening, processing information using auditory as well as visual input:

- Looks at teacher
- Responds to verbal cues
- Looks at interpreter
- Also sometimes re-interprets for the deaf student who uses ASL

The teacher is unaware of this.

Some 'demands' are systemic and embedded in the structure and constructs of the educational system.

What Would You Do?

Imagine yourself as the interpreter, D/deaf student(s) and teacher/hearing students in question. Put yourself into their "thought worlds."

What are the challenges you might face that may or may not be included here? Do you notice any other job requirements or something you feel triggers a response?

Example: if you were interpreting, what would your control(s) be to the demand of the two students using different modes of communication? What were other controls that might exist in this setting (for example, the fact that the students have access to the teacher's notes, power point slides, and textbook).

If you do something, what might the outcome be? Example: choose to sign in ASL. Student using SEE doesn't understand your interpretation (negative consequence?). Student using ASL does (positive consequence).

Would you need to then follow up and do something else? (respond to a new element, a new or resulting demand created by your decision, or control - the SEE student not understanding?). Would there be a need for a new control?

Categorizing Demands (EIPI or Environmental, Interpersonal, Paralinguistic and Intrapersonal)

Environmental: Goal of the environment, physical surroundings, personnel and clientele, terminology

Goals of the school, teacher, deaf students, interpreter, as perceived and stated by the interpreter:

- Teacher's goal was to explain the activity of the day and to have the students do the activity, and to encourage the students to use their "creative mind" to figure out how to solve a problem. The teacher wanted the students to leave with an understanding of the concept learned throughout the year by completing an experiential part of a regular lecture class.
- Students' goals were to go to each station, get the task done, get the information necessary for a good grade.
- Interpreter's goals were to interpret the teacher's explanations and have the deaf students understand (to support the teacher's goal, goal of the lesson), to try to get the information out there in a way that was correct or complete, 'put out a good product.'
- The school's goal is to provide the best education to the students with what they have available.
- Mentor helped restate the goal of the environment to be "to inform, educate."
- The classroom is noisy; the hearing students are talking, shouting. Each station contains concepts embedded within concepts (progressive build of terminology), (also an Interpersonal Demand)

Personnel/Clientele:

- 30-40 students, one teacher's aide (not involved with class)
- 2 deaf students
- 2 interpreters
- Teacher, walking around the room while talking (also Interpersonal/Paralinguistic demand)
- Terminology: "natural selection", "genotype", "phenotype", "predator", PTC paper

Interpersonal Demands: Challenges or requirements that relate to the interactions of consumers, communication style and goals, communication flow.

- The two deaf students using different modes of communication, ASL and SEE sign.
- The team interpreter doesn't have information missed or skewed when looked to for a feed.
- When the interpreter in the study is in the "off" chair (not interpreting), the team interpreter looks over frequently for feeds of missed/unknown vocabulary and utterances.
- When the teacher explains each station, the deaf students look over to that station and away from the interpreters. The teacher is unaware of this.
- When there is commotion the deaf students look over to see what happened.
- The deaf student who uses SEE is actively listening, processing information in an auditory as well as visual manner.
- Deaf students do not provide or decide on vocabulary choices with the interpreters
- Deaf students do not interrupt if they miss something or do not understand
- Each station contains concepts embedded within concepts (complexity of content – interaction of demands with the still-developing skills/controls of the interpreter)

Paralinguistic Demands: Expressive skills/tendencies of the deaf students, hearing students and teacher

The teacher is speaking very quickly, the teacher interrupts her explanation to the students to respond to individual questions, to reprimand students who are talking, shouting, walking on desks, and to respond to requests to use the bathroom, go to the office. The students are talking to each other while the teacher is talking. The students are talking while walking around and getting up on the desks, etc.

The deaf student who uses SEE sometimes "interprets" for the deaf student who uses ASL.

Intrapersonal Demands: Interpreter's feelings or thoughts about the assignment stressors, dynamics, safety, physical needs. Desire to interpret well for her videotape of this work today to use with her mentor, strong feelings about the difficulty of working in this class, concern about the deaf students getting all of the "important information."

The Next Step: Decisions or Controls

Controls that sound "inefficient" or may seem more like demands, such as "new interpreter", "first year interpreter", "interpreter with deaf parents" can be seen as nearly or almost neutral. It is in the interaction with demands that they may move from neutral to being a resource or asset, or become a resulting demand, and are truly understood in the light of the demands and follow up that may be required in response to the demand/control interaction. The interpreter decides to narrate an interchange between teacher and student (instead of interpreting it directly) - a response to three demands:

1. Fast paced speech
2. Frequent diversions by the teacher/students
3. Internal pressure to control her own attitude about this class (would be easier to "stay neutral" while narrating, by her report)

Looks to team for feeds of information missed, not heard, skewed, etc. Interprets "linearly and adds in some visuals (classifiers) to make it clear" to both deaf students.

Example of a linguistic control: (video sample not included here)

English: "You are being chased by a saber toothed tiger, reach a cliff and jump without a running start." Interpreter signs =- CL – CLIFF (omission and skewed figure-ground, doesn't show the other side of the cliff). Fingerspells "C-L-I-F-F (close to body) and C-L-I-F-F (further away from body).

Goal: to make it visual for the ASL student and also keep it linear for student who used SEE. The interpreter felt that the linguistic control was incomplete. Misunderstanding that the person jumped off the cliff and not to safety on the other side of the adjacent ledge.

Example response to the demand of specialised vocabulary: interpreters ask the deaf students, who decline, and so interpreters decide signs for natural selection.

- Interpreter prompts student to ask teacher directly when they have a question.
- Interpreter stays seated in her chair, does not accompany teacher around to stations.
- Interpreter decides to "hold onto" information while the students look over at the station and then back to interpreter.
- Interpreter does not know SEE beyond a few indicators of suffixes as they occur in English (-ing, -ment, -tion, etc.).
- Interpreter has a "decent background and comfort level with science".
- SEE student has an interest in health and science (this may be a demand that is "not demanding", depending on the interaction).
- Interpreter says she is "deciding what to keep and what to throw away" in response to several demands, by not interpreting "stuff that seemed superfluous, moot points...so students could get what they needed out of it".
- When the team interpreter was working, signs/information that was missed, missing or skewed were given.
- The class has been studying genotypes and phenotypes in previous classes, with the same interpreters.
- Interpreter reminded herself that today's information would be explained, then seen (students would have other means to get the information so not solely reliant upon the interpretation), teachers give the deaf student copies of power point slides.
- Interpreter has background knowledge of the situation: deaf students learn signs from each other; sometimes have note takers. The students try to take their own notes (this could be a demand as well – competing visual demands).

- The interpreter reminded herself that the deaf students are more visual learners – lessening the reliance for comprehension on the interpreted verbal explanation of the stations alone.
- Felt that the deaf students understood the role of the interpreter.
- Both interpreters encouraged the teacher to speak directly to the deaf students.
- The interpreter monitored her attitude about class via self-talk before class "it won't be as bad as last time – won't be hell like last time."
- Considered asking for help by having a lead teacher or academic counselor to come in and help gauge how well the interpretation in this situation was working for the deaf students.
- Requested a Deaf or Native ASL user as a Language Model for instruction for deaf students.

Discussion and Analysis of an Unresolved Ethical Dilemma

In applying this approach, the emphasis was to pull out one main demand that was most "ethically stressful" (Dean, 2001) to the interpreter, and go deeper into the process for an analysis of the decision, consequences, resulting demands, and whether or not there would be a need for more controls or different decisions.

The control chosen was the interpreter's decision to narrate an interchange between the teacher and one hearing student in a side conversation (to describe and summarise the interchange, pointing to and directing eye gaze to the interaction, stating that the teacher was annoyed with the student's constant questioning).

The dilemma: the interpreter's feeling was that she might have been more ethically correct to interpret the interchange instead of describing what was going on, for several reasons:

- She wanted to interpret everything but didn't' because it was "too much."
- Concern that she may have inserted her own opinion as to the nature of the interchange - was it annoyance? Was it that the student's asking too many questions caused the teacher's reaction?

- Concerned that interpreting rather than narrating would have provided a teaching moment for the students to see what happens if you ask too many questions of this teacher (students could not receive the experience and take meaning from it for themselves).
- This concern was in conjunction with another ethical dilemma, that of not letting her own annoyance with the situation become apparent in her interpreting. The interpreter felt that if she narrated instead of interpreted she'd be able to be more "neutral".

The next step in the DC-S once demands and controls and D/C interactions had been fleshed out sufficiently would be to look at the situation using the D-C-C-RD sequence: Demand, Control option applied, Consequence, Resulting Demand (new demand created by a negative consequence or less than successful outcome), assessment of need for any new control.

Demand Constellation she is responding to: fast paced speech, teacher's frequent side conversations with other students, noisy classroom, the interpreter's own attitude about class, etc.

Control: Narrate the side conversation between teacher and hearing student in which student is being reprimanded for asking too many questions "TEACHER - IX - ANNOY (8-HAND twist at temple) IX student "shake finger at".

Consequences: (positive) students get course content information (positive) interpreter manages the demands (negative) students miss out on a "learning moment" by not having access to the content of the conversation. The interpreter left with an unresolved ethical dilemma, still concerned about it one year later.

Resulting Demand: Interpreter doesn't feel there are any new demands created. Decides not to seek alternate control option(s)

Interpreter's response: "When my skills improved, or in a college class, I would have interpreted it. I wouldn't have changed the control after all. The students were familiar with this dynamic; often interpreted this type of interaction any time there were 'even a few seconds' to do so."

Given this constellation of demands, concurrent demands, not all required a response, yet affecting the priority of control options and cognitive load on the interpreters and deaf students.

Example: decoding information, expectations and instructions

Demand 1: One student uses SEE, a linear system following English word order. Deaf student is also listening (wears hearing aids).

Demand 2: One student uses ASL, a spatial - visual language. Stated challenge/goal of the interpreter: to linguistically "hit somewhere in between" the 2 different languages of the deaf students.

Control 1: produce an interpretation that followed the English output of the teacher, to interpret on a lexical level, in a more "linear" fashion.

Control 2: include classifiers as much as possible

In Conclusion

An educational interpreter is often on the "front lines" of a system that may have uninformed consumer(s), and an administration, educational system, and parents which have goals that differ from, and may restrict the efficiency or effectiveness of, the interpreter. The interpreter then, may be attempting to respond to one particular set of demands with particular controls, often unaware of her own decision making process, the demands she is encountering (overt and collective) and resources available to her. The hiring bodies often do not recognise the professional standards and professional needs of interpreters. When the amount of responsibility outweighs the options for response, the resulting stress can have a tremendous impact on the work product, well-being and morale of an interpreter and is detrimental to the successful education of deaf students.

Issues that surround the students and interpreters include, but are not limited to:

- Teacher preparation, education on deafness and interpreting.

- Class size.
- Teachers' workload.
- The social and emotional demands of high school and the interaction of such with minority status.
- Administration juggling personnel, legislative, budgetary issues.
- Hiring of interpreters while still in intensive skill development phases.
- Deaf students with language gaps.
- Parents without ready access to communication with their deaf child, information and support services.

The Demand Control Schema when applied to the interpreting product directly, supports the achievement of competencies for educational interpreters. It might then be applied as well, to help the interpreter maintain her role responsibilities, to function as a fellow professional (on a par with other staff and faculty, other professionals present), and engage in dialogues aimed at sharing the responsibility for the education of deaf students.

Future Considerations

Further dialogic analysis with this interpreter might include critical elements not considered in this presentation:
- Identification of pre-assignment and post-assignment controls
- Use of the ethics spectrum to discuss the range of controls from liberal to conservative, to act or not act and consequences
- Application of the Demand - Control - Consequence - Resulting Demand - New Control analysis in greater depth
- Sharing the process of evaluation of analysis - accuracy of assessing the demands/controls as a learning tool for mentors
- Case presentations shared amongst members of a study group preparing for certification
- Further consideration of the "Thought Worlds" of the classroom teacher and deaf students (and of the context of high school and the social/emotional demands on the students)

Acknowledgments

The interpreter in this case study, at the conclusion of the process, shared her appreciation of the chance to "unpack" the situation. She was awarded the NIC in January, 2008. This author extends her congratulations and deep appreciation for her generosity and willingness to share her process to further the profession.

Additionally, endless appreciation is extended to Patty Lessard, for, without her support, her mentoring and sharing of opportunities, this author would not have ventured into the process of presenting this work. Robyn Dean has provided endless hours of mentorship and instructional support and continues to provide deep inspiration to this author and to the many interpreters, deaf and hearing, in search of means to discuss and develop our work together.

Bibliography

Dean, R. K. & Pollard, R. Q., (2001). *Application of Demand-Control Theory to Sign Language Interpreting: Implications for Stress and Interpreter Training*, Journal of Deaf Studies and Deaf Education, 6 (1), 1-14.

Dean, R. K., Davis, J., Barnett, H., Graham, L..E., Hammond, L. Hinchey, K. (2003) January, Training Medically Qualified Interpreters: New Approaches, New Applications, Promising Results. VIEWS, 20; 1, 10-12.

Dean, R. K., Pollard, R. Q., English, M.A. (2004). *Observation-Supervision in Mental Health Interpreter Training.* In E.M. Maroney (Ed.), CIT: Still Shining After 25 Years (pp. 55-75). (Proceedings of the 15th national convention of the Conference of Interpreter Trainers (CIT). Monmouth, OR: CIT.

Dean, R. K., Pollard, R.Q., Davis, J., Griffin, M., LaCava, C., Morrison, B.,Parmir, J., Smith, A., Storme, S & Suback, L. (2004*). The Demand-Control Schema: Effective Curricular Implementation.* In E.M. Maroney (Ed.), CIT: Still Shining After 25 Years (pp. 55-75). (Proceedings of the 15th national convention of the Conference of Interpreter Trainers (CIT). Monmouth, OR: CIT.

Dean, R. K. & Pollard, R. Q., (2006). From *Best Practice to Best Practice Process: Shifting Ethical Thinking and Teaching.* In E.M. Maroney, (Ed.), A New Chapter in Interpreter Education: Accreditation, Research and Technology. (Proceedings of the 16th national convention of the Conference of Interpreter Trainers (CIT). Monmouth, OR: CIT.

Witter-Merithew, Anna and Leilani J. Johnson, *Toward Competent Practice: Conversations with Stakeholders* pp. 45 - 51, Registry of Interpreters for the Deaf, Inc. 2005

Resource texts the author has not directly referenced which influenced this work:

Shaw, R., (1997) *Many Stones to Form an Arch: Cooperation and Consideration as the Cornerstones of Successful Interpretation*, based on a keynote presentation at the RID Region IV conference, 1996. Journal of Interpretation, RID 7-1-97.

Kinsella, T., (1997) *Beyond Correction and Critique: Working in Teams* (first published in NH RID newsletter). Journal of Interpretation, RID 7-1-97.

Educational Interpreting: Multiple Perspectives on our Work From Deaf students, teachers, administrators and parents, by Debra Russell and Jane McLeod

Introduction

Increasingly throughout North America, Europe, and Australia, Deaf children are accessing education in their local schools via an inclusive education model. The majority of these Deaf students use Sign Language interpreters, thus experiencing 'mediated education' (i.e., the information from a teacher and student is mediated through an interpreter). Although the inclusion model has received support for its ability to improve the success of students with disabilities, and provide them with opportunities they would otherwise not have access to, Deaf children typically fall behind their hearing peers both academically and socially (Russell, 2007; Schick, Marschark, & Spencer, 2006). In addition, there is little research to date to verify the value of this model for Deaf learners, calling its validity into question.

Administrators often assume that hiring a Sign Language interpreter ensures that the Deaf child has a learning experience the same as a non-deaf child. However, the vast majority of Deaf students in the United States and New Zealand do not received an equitable educational experience compared to their hearing peers, due to the lack of qualified interpreters employed by school districts (La Bue,1998; Locker-McKee & Biederman, 2003; Winston, 2004). In addition, although Deaf children appear to have access to the language of instruction through interpretation, much of this linguistic input does not allow for meaningful inclusion, nor does it allow for Deaf students to fully access the learning environment. As a result, Deaf students often fall behind their hearing peers academically, and are more likely to report social isolation, non-participation, and academic exclusion (Russell, 2007). In effect, Deaf students are mostly *physically* placed in the inclusive environment, thus leading to an *illusion of inclusion.*

The intent of this paper to describe a national study to identify the key issues shaping the education of Deaf students within the inclusive setting. It is also intended to introduce standards and recommendations for enhancing the inclusive setting for Deaf learners. Canadian research on the inclusive setting has thus far has not included the perspectives of students, parents, teachers, interpreters, and administrators. These, however, are critical to the understanding and improvement of mediated education within Canada. By including these 'voices' with the current literature in North America, Australia, and Europe, a more complete and realistic picture of the inclusive educational model may emerge.

Participants

The participants discussed in this paper include 13 Sign Language interpreters, two deaf-blind intervenors, 15 Deaf students, ten parents, 56 teachers (ten with no training working with deaf/hard-of-hearing students, and 46 either teachers with experience working with Deaf children and/or children with special needs), and four administrators. Both urban and rural school districts were included in the current study. Of the Sign Language interpreters, ten possessed some form of formal interpreter education (completed a one or two year program), and two had no formal interpreter education. This paper reports the themes that emerged from the interview data and online surveys.

Results

The following section identifies the themes and perceptions that emerged from the interviews. Student and teacher perceptions of working with interpreters are discussed first, teacher perceptions of working with deaf students, followed by parent and administrator opinions.

Student Perceptions

When interviewed regarding the quality of interpreting services they received within the classroom, students reported inconsistencies in the hiring of interpreters, as well as a lack of qualified interpreters to work within the educational environment. They also indicated that the interpreter's ability to mediate the classroom lecture played a role in their understanding of material. According to the students, interpreters who seem able to easily mediate conversation between the teacher and student provide a more thorough, and interactive learning experience. Those who struggle with the material, and appear under-qualified to work within the educational environment, hinder the students' ability to learn.

In addition, students who reside within urban centres appear to have greater access to qualified interpreters, as compared to rural students. Students in high school also reported that they felt greater access to more qualified interpreters, whereas students in elementary schools and junior high programs described working with assistants who were not qualified.
Other themes emerging from the data include:

Interpreters education programs – adult focused

Students suggested that the interpreters with whom they worked often seemed uncomfortable working with children, and do not seem to understand how to behave around children. This is supported by the literature describing interpreter-training programs as being oriented largely towards the education of adults, and that there is a lack of specialised training for interpreters to work within the inclusive environment (Schick, Marschark, & Spencer, 2006). This highlights students' belief that there should be more specialised training for interpreters who work within the educational system, so that they may be better able to relate and interact on a more compatible level to younger students.

Linguistic skills and interpreting processes

One student, who is enrolled in the gifted and talented program, reported that the interpreters struggled to understand the content in the classroom, despite having strong interpreting skills. This is also supported by previous findings that interpreters are often certified by general education programs, and are not instructed on specialised areas within the education system (Russell, 2007). This student reported frustration that their education was impeded due to a poor inclusive environment.

Preparation for classes

Interestingly, students within the junior high and high school setting reported that they could identify when an interpreter seemed comfortable with the class material, and understood its context fully. This was largely shown from the interpreter's ease of signing and ability to convey the content of the lecture. These students also indicated that when changes of interpreters were needed (regular interpreter ill, or schedule changes occur within the school), the replacing interpreter is often unqualified/lacking the ability to convey the message of classroom interactions. As a result, these students indicated that the lack of proper interpretation affects their ability to participate in the classroom.

Use of multimedia

Surprisingly, all students interviewed reported that teachers did not use media that was captioned. They indicated that if this media were used within the classroom, they would experience a more enriched learning environment. Students in junior high reported that interpreters were taken from their classes in order to offer interpreting services to Deaf high school students enrolled in diploma exams.

Social connections

Students reported that, after Grade 3, they felt as though they did not have friends or meaningful connections to other non-Deaf students.

Group discussions – Exclusion

Across all interviews, Deaf students reported that they were unable to participate in group discussions and debates within the classroom. This experience is described as challenging, due to the difficulty for the interpreters when mediating the pace of discussion/interaction amongst multiple speakers. Interestingly, interpreters themselves reported that they frequently ask teachers to moderate classroom discussions, so to provide the Deaf students with greater opportunity to participate and respond. Some interpreters even identified the need to interrupt the classroom teacher during these discussions, in order to facilitate a more appropriate pace for the Deaf student. Both interpreters and Deaf students, however, reported frustration with this style of teaching/learning process, as it typically leads to a lack of understanding and poor academic achievement for the Deaf student.

Teacher Perceptions

The following themes emerged when teachers working with Deaf students in the inclusive educational model were interviewed:

Teachers' perceptions of interpreter qualifications

When asked to describe educational interpreters with whom they'd worked, teachers reported that qualifications and professionalism varied considerably amongst interpreters. They indicated that some interpreters present themselves as professionals, are adequately prepared for classroom content, seek out advice/information regarding lectures from the teacher, and appear genuinely interested in the students' academic progress. Other interpreters appear disinterested in the teaching/learning environment, engage in limited interaction with both the student and/or teacher, and perform only the basic requirements necessary for the position.

Some teachers have also reported that they have experienced interpreters "lecturing" to them about how to work with the interpreter, with little focus on how to best accommodate the needs of the Deaf student. One teacher reported a preference of working with "[interpreters who view themselves as part of the teaching team, and are willing to support teacher/student interactions in a positive way]". Therefore, teachers appear to be reporting discrepancies in expectations of the interpreter within the inclusive environment, which ultimately compensates the education of the Deaf student.

The teachers in this sample identified that they did not know who supervised the interpreter, how they were assessed at time of hiring, or how the interpreters were scheduled. Despite this, a large percentage of teachers are very satisfied with the interpreters that work within the school (50%). Others reported that they are satisfied (15%) or not satisfied (35%). Many teachers indicated that they are unsure of what is expected of the interpreter within the inclusive setting, and are therefore using personal tactics/intuition to assess the interpreter's performance (Russell, 2007), as well as assessments performed by administrators.

Communication with Deaf students

Teachers that were included in this study indicated that they are able to fairly easily communicate with the Deaf students, although the method through which they communicated depended on their familiarity with signing, and ability to mediate communication between the interpreter and Deaf student. Although the majority of individuals were primarily English speaking, 53% of the teachers indicated that they know how to sign moderately well, and some know how to sign fluently. Only a small portion of the teachers, however, indicated that they did not know how to sign at all/could only sign somewhat (13%). Of those that were familiar with signing, they used the following to communicate with students in their classrooms: English signs in English word order, American Sign Language, fingerspelling, combination of mouthing words/signing, and Signed Exact English (SEE).

Teachers fluent in signing communicate fairly easily with the Deaf students, although they reported it was more limited compared to their communication with hearing students. Teachers that were familiar with signing reported better ability to assess the students' progress in the classroom, their level of interaction with their peers, and the qualification level of the interpretation service provided to the interpreter (Russell, 2007). Teachers who were not familiar with signing, however, reported much greater difficulty when communicating with students. They felt a much greater dependency on the interpreter, and reported greater frustration when conveying a message to the Deaf student.

More support and specialised training needed

Despite having general teaching strategies/personal tactics, the majority of teachers felt as though they lacked the support and training to accommodate Deaf students within the inclusive setting, nor how to effectively work with an interpreter. Many expressed frustration with consistently having to modify their method of teaching for the deaf student, and concern for their lack of training do provide an appropriate educational environment for the deaf student. Other concerns included their limited access to specialised media equipment within their schools, and their personal lack of understanding of how to operate the equipment. Teachers recommended a desire for more professional development workshops, training opportunities, and resources to support their work with Deaf students and/or interpreters.

Some teachers also reported a desire to access external consulting services, which could provide assistance and guidance in supporting Deaf learner. One teacher indicated that she is accessing such services, but can only do so three times in the academic year. She expressed that these services should be provided on a regular basis, to provide a more interactive form of support that teachers may access when needed. These external supports, however, are funded by the school's budget; these restrictions therefore limit the amount of support available to teachers.

Understanding of signing and the interpreter's role within the inclusive setting

Surprisingly, not all of the teachers interviewed indicated that there is an interpreter hired within their school. In 18% of the schools, there is no interpretation service provided for the deaf students, and 9% of schools employ an interpreter on only some occasions. Additionally, individuals hired as interpreters are not always qualified. Only 68% of schools have professional interpreters, and 27% hire signers only. Some teachers indicated that they are not aware of the difference between an interpreter and a signer.

In schools that hire interpreters, most often only one interpreter is employed; although a small portion of schools recognise the need for more interpreters, and will hire over five. Despite these interpreters that are employed within the school, only 32% of teachers indicate the interpreters are available for the students to participate in extracurricular activities, 41% indicate that the interpreters are not available for the students to participate in extracurricular activities, and 20% indicate that they are only available sometimes (Russell, 2008, unpublished data). Therefore, this limits the deaf students' ability to develop relationships with peers and engage in school activities outside of the classroom setting.

Teachers also recommended that Deaf students should be placed in classrooms with experienced teachers, particularly those who have worked with students with special needs. Teachers in this sample emphasised the need for teachers to learn basic signing, so that they may communicate with the student in some manner and provide them with feedback. They suggested that this would facilitate an understanding of the interpreter's role and their performance within the classroom. Nine of the teachers interviewed, however, did not see this as important.

Self-esteem and social connections of Deaf Students

In general, teachers view Deaf students as being socially delayed compared to their hearing peers: they perceive Deaf students as being socially inhibited when part of an inclusive educational model, and many expressed a desire for the deaf student to spend more time interacting with others. Interestingly, teachers said that they see their d/Deaf students interacting equally with both their deaf (34.8%) and non-deaf classmates (34.8%). The difference between these interactions, however, is the *quality* of interaction that occurs; that is, most teachers expressed concern that deaf students were unable to form meaningful relationships with their non-deaf peers. Most teachers attribute this to the limitations of interpretation, social isolation, and stereotyping of students who are deaf. They also said that some hearing students feel uncomfortable talking with the Deaf student through an interpreter, who is "like another teacher" (Russell, 2008, unpublished data).

As a result, teachers perceive deaf children as becoming prone to a decreased self-esteem and confidence compared to their hearing peers. 22% of teachers indicate that the deaf student's self-esteem is low, 42% indicated it was satisfactory, 31% indicated it was high, and only 4% said the deaf students' self-esteem was very high (Russell, 2008, unpublished data). The participants often commented on how they felt that these students' social interactions were lagging behind that of their non-deaf peers. During recess and lunch breaks, teachers said that deaf students are most likely to be found with a small group of people (2-3 people) (69%) or with only one friend (21%). Less likely would be to find the deaf student alone (7%) or within a large group (4+ people) (2%) (Russell, 2008, unpublished data). Therefore, although few deaf students are completely isolated from their peers, teachers indicated that the deaf students are socially limited compared to their hearing peers, due to the barrier created by interpretation and stereotyping of deaf students.

Methods of communication with other students

Despite this, teachers feel that the majority of students do try to communicate with hearing peers (87%). Those that interact with their hearing peers on a frequent basis are perceived by their teachers to be extremely successful academically and socially within the inclusive education models (Russell, 2007). Most teachers felt that the deaf students varied their approach of communication in order to remain social within the class, and although often easily frustrated, made efforts to communicate with their non-deaf peers (Russell, 2008, unpublished data). Non-conventional methods of communication are also useful for communication with deaf students in an inclusive setting. These include text based messaging (MSN/Text messaging) (33%), and Pen/Paper (49%), fingerspelling, and relying on the interpreter (7%).

Administrator Perceptions

The following themes emerged from the interviews with principals and administrators:

Inclusion works

In general, administrators felt that the school was completely accessible to the Deaf students enrolled in an inclusive setting. They also reported that the students were 'well integrated' within the classroom, and were socially on par with their hearing peers. When asked to define critical improvements needed to create an accessible learning environment for Deaf learners, principals responded that hiring more interpreters was all that was needed. Two out of the four administrators were pleased with the work of interpreters.

Supervision

When asked to define who is in the best position to supervise and mentor interpreters, all administrators indicated that they provide effective supervision to all their staff, regardless of specialised function. None of these administrators, however, had previous certification and/or qualifications in assessing interpreters.

Team interpreting

Large schools often employ teams of interpreters, to provide full access and availability of interpreters for the Deaf students. Surprisingly, the administrators interviewed in this study reported that they felt one interpreter was sufficient in the school, and that a team of interpreters was not necessary within the school. None of the principals reported knowledge of incidence levels of repetitive strain injuries among interpreters, or the issues shaping quality interpretation. They felt, in general, that one interpreter would be sufficient to support the needs of Deaf students who attend that school, similar to educational assistants.

Difficult, expensive helpers

Three out of the four administrators in this study reported that they viewed the interpreters as difficult and demanding. One of the principals described that they are 'expensive helpers', suggesting that an educational assistant would be a more cost-effective assistant for the Deaf student. Two principals questioned the need for interpreters to be in a separate category per the union agreement; they elaborated that by creating a separate category for interpreters, they would see their role within the educational environment in rigid parameters.

All administrators expressed concern over the inflexibility of some interpreters, and how this does not serve educational settings effectively. In general, administrators appear to be describing a discrepancy between their expectations of the interpreter within the school (effective interpreting, maintaining low-costs for interpreting services, inclusion within the classroom), and what is actually feasible for both the interpreter and the deaf student within the classroom.

Parent Perceptions

The following themes emerged from the interviews with parents:

Confusion of the interpreter's role

Parents in this sample said that they did not have a common understanding of what role the interpreter plays in the learning/teaching environment, and how their work supports that of the teacher. Most parents indicated that they use basic or family-created signs, and learn more signing techniques as needed (i.e., when the student surpasses their level of signing; when they are no longer able to effectively communicate with their child). Despite this, they are commonly not aware of the role the interpreter plays within a classroom setting.

In addition, parents expressed confusion regarding interpreter qualifications that are necessary to work within an educational setting. They identified a lack of ability to monitor the quality of interpreters working with their children, and the education their children were receiving as a result. A few parents identified times in which the school districts had hired an unqualified interpreter, which negatively impacted their child's educational experience and performance. Despite this, they are also aware of the limited availability of qualified educational interpreters in both urban and rural areas.

As a result, many parents indicated that they would hire any interpreter who claimed to have some knowledge of interpreting, if they felt that this would be of assistance for their child. During an interview, one parent described this experience as the following: '..We know the [interpreter] is not qualified, but the school says that is all they can afford, so [we think] it is the best that is possible....anyone is better than no one!' These comments reflect the general lack of support received within the inclusive setting, reported by the parents of Deaf students.

Money restrictions within the inclusive setting

Several parents also outlined school board policies stating that "Deafness is a low incidence disability", and are unable to expend large monetary value towards a single child's needs. Therefore, parents feel that their children are receiving a decreased quality of education, due to lack of funding in the educational system. Parents expressed confusion about funding decisions made by the school boards, indicating that Deaf students are ranked lower compared to other children with special needs. One parent described this experience:

> "How does the number of students take away from what the individual child needs – I don't understand how my child can go without interpreting services so that funds can be diverted to a group of students who share the same form of disability!"

Parents therefore report mostly negative support from school districts, and lack of direction for ways of increasing support within the educational system. Others expressed the need to improve the gaps within the inclusive educational setting, including increasing availability of interpreting services, monitoring the qualifications of interpreters hired within the schools, and increasing social supports for Deaf students within the inclusive setting.

Need for advocacy towards change for the inclusive setting

All parents interviewed felt that their child was receiving a decreased educational experience compared to hearing children. Parents in rural areas indicated that there are few resources for their child, limiting their ability to access qualified interpreters when needed. Those in urban settings reported that although there are increased resources available, many of these resources were unreliable or unqualified to work within the educational system.

When interviewed, some parents described their attempts to promote improvements to the inclusive setting to both Canadian administrators and government agencies. Parents described the response received as "….patronising…..[giving them] the impression that they were to remain quiet, and be thankful for the level of service they are currently receiving". Those who do take the initiative to advocate for their Deaf child, feel that their feedback is not welcome. One parent described worrying about their child, due to the uncertainty they associate with their educational experience. 'I worry about what will happen for my child – will they get a job….[will they] go to college?' The parents therefore seemed largely concerned for the welfare of their child and their long-term success (career and/or education), and how to implement changes within the inclusive setting to overcome these obstacles.

Intervening services for Deaf-Blind students

Intervening services have recently been implemented within the school system; parents who have children who are both Deaf and blind expressed feelings of relief that their child was receiving more support in the classroom. One parent indicated, however, that administrators hold lower academic expectations for these children, and are therefore challenged less academically. One parent described Deaf-Blind children being placed within the same class, despite differences in their academic performance. The parent felt that this was done solely to decrease costs of hiring intervening services, and forces the intervener to work at the pace of the 'slower' student. The parent described this as "… increasing the frustration for my child, and decreases their motivation in the educational climate".

Role models

Parents indicated their Deaf children often viewed the interpreters and intervenors as role models, given that very often, they are the only ones who can have direct communication with the child during the day. Parents therefore expressed a desire for the interpreters and intervenors to present themselves as more positive, professional, and respectful of Deaf culture. One parent indicated that, since her child has no close friendships with girls her age, and lacks peer role models, the influence of the interpreter's role is of great importance. Parents are therefore raising concern that the interpreters working within the educational system should become more sensitive to their role and the impact they play in the Deaf students' lives.

Preliminary Conclusions

Based on this preliminary data, it appears that gaps within the inclusive setting need to be addressed, in order to create a meaningful educational experience for the Deaf child. This includes addressing the concerns of parents, teachers, administrators, and Deaf students themselves.

Major themes that emerged from the current data include the following:

Confusion of the interpreter's role within the educational setting

It appears that there are varying expectations amongst administrators, teachers, parents, and interpreters themselves of what is required by an interpreter working within an inclusive educational setting. Interpreters often describe the need to advocate for the student, remind the teacher to keep the pace of the class acceptable for the deaf student, and manage their role as an interpreter, so that the student may be successful both academically and socially. While this may benefit the Deaf student, administrators and teachers often feel that this attitude seems confrontational, and that their suggestions interfere with the regular pace hearing students desire.

In addition, most administrators are not aware of the importance of hiring multiple interpreters, which would provide more support within the school for deaf students, decrease the rate of burnout for interpreters working within the school, and to increase the availability for interpretation services for both classroom and extracurricular activities. Most administrators view the role of the interpreter similar to that of an educational assistant, and are unaware of the special needs of Deaf students within the inclusive setting. In addition, parents of Deaf children are largely unaware of the role the interpreter plays within the classroom, and express concern that their child does not receive a proper education.

Further discussion and communication regarding the interpreter's role is therefore necessary, so that the inclusive setting may best support and facilitate a learning environment for the Deaf student. In addition, teachers working with Deaf students are expressing a desire for more professional development opportunities and training workshops, so that they may best work with an interpreter in the classroom setting.

Standardised interpreter qualifications needed

Other issues emerging from the data suggest that many interpreters are not available to all Deaf students, and most interpreters are under-qualified to work within the educational setting. Since administrators and teachers are uncertain as to what quantifies an experienced interpreter, they instead rely on the interpreter's general performance in the classroom, and personal tactics to assess the interpreter. Unfortunately, the Deaf students' academic and social success is often compensated as a result of poor interpretation.

It is therefore necessary for administrators and school boards to implement more rigorous hiring practices for interpreters, and standardising the necessary requirements for those who are hired to work as interpreters within the inclusive setting. This may include requiring basic interpreter certification courses and proof of interpretation experience prior to being hired.

Addressing the academic and social gaps within the inclusive setting

Although teachers reported that Deaf students interact with their non-deaf peers, many teachers report that communication barriers exist, which may lead to fewer social opportunities, segregation, and poor self-esteem amongst Deaf students. In addition, teachers felt that the inclusive setting is not conducive for the Deaf students' learning, and information taught by the teacher may be lost through interpretation. This contradictory information provided by teachers clearly points to the *illusion of inclusion.*

The presence of an interpreter and other basic provisions in a mainstream classroom give the impression of full inclusion. However, teachers' own confessions reveal that inclusion may only be a façade. In order to address this, teachers need to be taught education and assessment strategies that will support d/Deaf students specialised needs.

Advocating needs of Deaf students

Despite these concerns, the inclusive setting does offer Deaf students opportunities that would otherwise not be available to them. Teachers felt that inclusion helps to decrease stereotypes and isolation of the students, allowing the deaf students to experience the same opportunities as non-deaf students, and help prepare the deaf students for a "real-world" situation. This experience may help to increase the deaf students' self-esteem and ability to interact with their non-deaf peers.

The results of this study show that most deaf students attempt to be social within the classroom setting, despite potential communication barriers that may occur when interacting with their non-deaf peers, and the frustration that results from trying to communicate through an interpreter. A large proportion of deaf students communicate with sign, highlighting the need for deaf students' to access quality interpreting within the inclusive setting. Unfortunately, not all schools hire interpreters for deaf students, and those that do, often hire unqualified interpreters. In addition, the interpreters are rarely available for the students to participate in extracurricular activities. This may limit the deaf students' ability to form meaningful relationships with their peers, and, as a result, may negatively impact their self-esteem.

Therefore, further research is necessary to improve the inclusive setting for Deaf students. Identifying their primary needs, as well as the concerns of their parents, may help administrators and teachers to create a more meaningful learning environment for the deaf student. In addition, advocating the needs of Deaf students within the school, as well as increasing knowledge of deaf culture within the school will help decrease stereotyping of Deaf students, and help improve their ability to socialise with peers in the classroom.

Conclusion

Despite the widespread use of the inclusive education model in Canada, little research has been done to investigate the effectiveness of this method. The research project described in this paper will obtain a global perspective of the inclusive education model in Canada, by obtaining data from deaf students, their parents, teachers and school administrators. It is also intended that the Canadian inclusive model be compared to that of North America, New Zealand, Australia, and Europe. Issues such as the quality of interpretation, teaching strategies, Deaf student's social and academic success, administrator perspectives, parental concerns, and misconceptions of interpretation have been explored with this data.

To date, data from various students, teachers, administrators, and parents that have been collected. The need for improved teacher/administrator education regarding interpreting services has been identified, as well as greater understanding of the interpreter's role within the inclusive setting. In addition, greater advocacy for the needs of deaf students and interpreters is necessary, so that more appropriate supports for Deaf students may be implemented in the school. More awareness of communication through interpretation is also needed, in order to improve teacher's ability to communicate to the deaf students, and so deaf students may form more meaningful relationships with their hearing peers.

The question that predominantly remains is "under what context or conditions does inclusion work best?" It appears that there are differing opinions amongst all parties, although most feel there are many opportunities to enhance the inclusive setting. Most individuals interviewed feel that more rigorous interpreter education and training is necessary, so that all Deaf students may receive equal opportunities within the classroom. This may also equip interpreters to work with the demands of the teaching/learning environment, and to work more effectively with children from five to eighteen years of age. In addition, improved recognition of the need to hire qualified interpreters, who can provide access to the language of the classroom, is necessary.

It also seems clear that teacher orientation/specialised workshops are required, in addition to understanding of adaptations needed within the inclusive setting (i.e., slightly slower pace, more articulation of speech during group discussions, more interaction with the interpreter), so that Deaf students may fully participate in classroom discussion and interactions. The need for more visual aids within the classroom is also recommended, which will enhance the learning experience for students who cannot hear auditory messages of teachers.

In order for Deaf students to truly receive an inclusive education, gaps in administrators' perceptions and teacher education need to be addressed, and the appropriate supports need to be implemented. There is also an overwhelming need for dialogue among all stakeholders, to facilitate improvements to the current inclusive setting. Once these steps, opportunities for Deaf students within the inclusive setting may be established, so that they may experience a more meaningful and complete educational experience.

References

La Bue, M.A. (1998). *Interpreted education: A study of Deaf students' access to the content and form of literacy instruction in a mainstreamed high school English class*. Retrieved from ProQuest Dissertations & Thesis: Full Text. (AAT 9830061).

Locker-McKee, R. & Biederman, Y. (2003). The construction of learning contexts for Deaf bilingual learners. In R. Bernard & T. Glynn (Eds.) *Bilingual children's language and literacy development* (pp. 194 – 225). England: Multilingual Matters.

Russell, D. (2007). What do others think of our work? Deaf students, teachers, administrators and parents' perspectives on educational interpreting. In Cynthia Roy (Ed.). *Diversity and Community in the Worldwide Sign Language Interpreting Profession: Proceedings of the second World Association of Sign Language Interpreters 2007 Conference* (pp. 34-38). Gloucester, UK: Douglas McLean Publishing.

Russell, D. (2008). [Access to education: Deaf students in inclusive settings]. Unpublished raw data.

Schick, B. S., Marschark, M., & Spencer, P. E. (2006). Advances in the Sign Language development of deaf children [electronic resource]. Oxford; New York: Oxford University Press.

Winston, E.A. (Ed.). (2004). *Educational interpreting: How it can succeed.* Washington, DC: Gallaudet Press.

Summary of the conference discussion

The discussion began with a thread on mainstream educational placements and the view held by some that this is the 'least restrictive environment'. Many deaf students describe a tremendous sense of social and linguistic isolation in mainstream settings. Is not social isolation itself restrictive?

As the paper proves, there is a distinction between the administration's perspective ('school was completely accessible' and 'Deaf students are well integrated with many friends') vs. what the Deaf students themselves describe as social isolation. The administrators in this survey 'don't see the need for two interpreters,' and viewed the interpreters as 'difficult and demanding' and 'inflexible.' Interpreters strive to establish clear boundaries so that all stakeholders can be more clear about their roles in 'mediated education,' and yet struggle with administrations which clearly have little understanding of what is needed to even attempt to make things work well in an interpreted environment.

There is a dearth of documented research on mainstreaming for deaf children, and in Canada Deaf children were enrolled in public school without any evidence at all. The challenge is to model a message of inclusion that is ' for whom and under what context' - and bringing people to look at all of the factors that must be present for 'real' education. So the challenge is to look at the child's linguistic, cognitive and social needs, and context changes - what support needs to be in place? Is a qualified interpreter enough? Do we need to have a critical mass of Deaf children in the school to allow for natural peer and social interaction opportunities? Do we need teachers who have been trained to work with Deaf learners to be doing the teaching or providing consulting to other teachers about adapting their strategies? What about Deaf role models and Deaf tutors? What a child needs in one year maybe very different next year and so on.

The opportunity to have incidental learning is important for all children. In order for this to happen, there needs to be a language rich environment. It does not follow that one particular setting is better than another, as there can be language impoverished situations in schools for the Deaf, in mainstream classes and in integrated classes. There have to be opportunities for the Deaf learner to talk about ideas with peers directly, which implies having more than one Deaf student in the school or finding opportunities outside of school for such conversations.

Another aspect of the presentation which puzzled delegates was the information on how all administrators questioned for Russell's research felt they could supervise and mentor interpreters, and 2 out of 4 were pleased with the work of the interpreters. Questions were raised on what basis these administrators were providing their answers. Similarly, the presentation stated that 9 out of 10 teachers didn't think it was important to learn basic signs when they have a deaf student in their class for a year.

In response, the presenter answered that administrators reported being able to supervise and mentor the interpreter just like any member of the staff. What seemed to be consistent with all the administrators is the notion that once they are able to successfully hire someone, they assume competency in that person. Their views on mentoring were that they provide information about the school and how to function within the school climate, which is not what the interpreters meant when they said they wanted mentoring. The two administrators who were pleased based their views on the fact that they didn't hear any complaints from or about the interpreters.

The teachers involved in the study reported having no orientation to teaching Deaf students and the changes they could make that might include Deaf students in more meaningful ways. The information they get from the interpreters is about interpreting do's and don't but nothing has focused on what they can do as good teachers to manage group discussions, to pause when there is a need to demonstrate and then talk, adjust the timing of their responses to students, or information about the Deaf student's language and learning experience, etc. One of the most experienced teachers who has also had significant experience with Deaf students and interpreters has learned to adapt and uses some great strategies. However, the school does not necessarily see that resource even within their teaching pool. As for basic signs, many of those teachers operate on the belief that the children can understand them when they speak and after all, that is why the interpreter is in the classroom.

Some teachers do collaborate and work well with interpreters, providing preparation materials, and making sure the interpreter is seen as part of the educational team. They and their students receive a better interpretation experience because of it. Providing quality interpretation is easier when everyone on the educational team has as their goal the student's learning.

The presentation indicated that it is obvious when an interpreter is well prepared for an assignment. Unfortunately, many interpreters do not seem to see this as a priority in their work. Some have the attitude that the interpreting work only happens when they are with the deaf person. But both within educational settings and elsewhere the work and interpreter puts in beforehand is crucial to the effectiveness within the lecture.

The presenter added some information on linguistic data and interviews with interpreters about their classroom work. Some of the data suggests that interpreters who have worked for several years in an educational setting assume they don't have to prep any more, as they know the curriculum. Or interpreters are doing what might be termed 'passive prep' - that is reading the material over quickly, but not engaging in any critical analysis about what the content looks like in a signed language, and how that might be structured with regard to ASL discourse. Looking at this from the perspective of metacognition, the data identified 6 distinct discourse functions that teachers use in classroom interaction, and it is clear how frequently interpreters are not able to realise those functions in their work. So on top of the prep, there are interpreters who are missing the whole purpose behind the teacher's talk. Things like sequencing strategies, offering feedback, scaffolding, posing questions that require bringing forward associated and background knowledge, peer teaching are either not present in the interpretation or done in such a way that the Deaf learner has no access to them. In educational settings it is essential to have interpreters who can do active preparation before hand and apply their own metacognitive skills to understanding the teacher's discourse as they are talking - and then to be able to offer those discourse structures in ways that are conventional in ASL. This is a hugely difficult task for an interpreter and requires a lot of skill.

One delegate raised the question whether responses to the study from teaching professionals indicated how they perceive their relationship with the interpreter in terms of equality, or inequality. Did they report that they viewed the interpreter as a fellow professional of equal status? So far the data would suggest that the majority of teachers do not see interpreters as their equals or members of the educational team. There are teachers who reported feeling judged by the interpreter and newly qualified teachers reported that they really were nervous having an other adult in the room with them when they were just getting their footing as teachers. Ultimately, the teachers reported that the only orientation they had to interpreting and working with a Deaf student came from the interpreter. Often that orientation was described as interpreters dictating what the teacher needed to do, without any dialogue about working as a team or the myriad of issues that impact a Deaf learner in an inclusive setting. So there is a great deal more that needs to happen around teacher orientation, and maybe this is best done by a teacher who knows about teaching diverse Deaf learners, in co-operation with the interpreter who can speak to their issues. But HOW to frame those issues is also a key learning for interpreters. In contrast, one of the very experienced teachers in the study, who has had several years of working with Deaf learners and interpreters reported that he/she can now identify the interpreters who work well in their classroom, and will request specific interpreters. This teacher clearly sees the interpreter as part of the educational team, and wants interpreters to be able to see themselves as more than conduits for his/her messages.

There is a need to address 'how to work with the teacher' during interpreter education programs. Many of the interpreters doing the work in the Canadian system are often new interpreters (0-5 years of experience) and are also often some of the youngest practitioners, who are just becoming young adults. There are many factors that can shape holding those conversations with the educational team, but some novice interpreters are ill-equipped for this role. What may be helpful is to have the conversations with teachers about what they might need, what their concerns might be about having an interpreter in the classroom, finding out what they think good teaching is, and so on, before interpreters talk about what they need and prescribe working practices for the teacher. For example, lawyers in one of the presenter's other conducted studies reported that they were overwhelmed with how the interpreters described what they would be doing and so on, while none of the interpreters asked the lawyers about what they needed from the interpreters. They commented that it wasn't a dialogue, but rather a monologue from the interpreter. This insight can apply to the school setting, and finding common language from the teacher's perspective can help build a good working relationship.

Ten years of bilingual deaf education in Norway – where are we? by Arnfinn Muruvik Vonen

Introduction

In 1997, deaf children in Norway received the right to Sign Language tuition and, thereby, to bilingual education involving Norwegian Sign Language (NSL) and Norwegian. This paper will give some information about this landmark event in deaf education in Norway and share some reflections concerning the situation a decade later. It will be argued that the introduction of bilingual deaf education into national legislation has had an important impact, but also that several central issues remain unsettled. I will also reflect upon the emergence of an anti-bilingual discourse connected with pediatric cochlear implantation.

The Act of Education and the Curriculum of 1997

The Ministry of Education recognised NSL as a language in the Report to the Storting [Parliament] No. 61 (1984-85), referring to the appearance of linguistic research on the language in the early 1980s:[1] "This research has shown that the Sign Language of the deaf must be equalled with other languages. When this Sign Language is now accepted as a language, this must have certain consequences for the education of deaf children."

After subsequent years of experimenting in the schools for the deaf, drafting of curricula and other preparatory activities, deaf children's legal right to bilingual education was finally introduced as a new section of the Regulation to the Act of the Compulsory School in

---

[1] "Denne forskinga har vist at teiknspråket til dei døve må jamstillast med andre språk. Når no dette teiknspråket blir akseptert som språk, må det få visse konsekvensar for opplæringa av døve barn."

1997. When a new Act of Education was passed in 1998, the right was included in the text of the Act itself:[1]

> "Pupils who have Sign Language as their first language, have the right to primary and lower secondary tuition both in the use of Sign Language and through the medium of Sign Language. [...]
> Children under compulsory school age who have a special need for Sign Language tuition, have the right to such tuition. [...]"
> (Act of Education, 1998-2000, section 2-6)

The introduction of the right to bilingual education for deaf children was an integrated part of a major curriculum reform in Norwegian education, Reform 97, which included a new Curriculum for the Compulsory School in Norway. The curriculum for deaf pupils was defined as identical with that of hearing pupils, with two exceptions: First, the subjects Norwegian, English and Music, in all of which sound plays an important role, were replaced by specially adapted subjects for deaf pupils. Second, deaf pupils were given additional lessons so that NSL could become a new, important subject.

In 2000, section 3-9 of the Act of Education gave deaf pupils in upper secondary education the right to bilingual education. In 2006, the next general curriculum reform for primary and secondary education continued the four special subjects for deaf pupils.

Among several other governmental actions taken in the 1990s to strengthen NSL's position, "See My Language" ["Se mitt språk"] should be mentioned. A 40-week NSL training programme for parents of deaf children, collaboratively financed by the social security system, the national education system and the municipalities in which the families live, it was introduced in 1996 and is, to my knowledge, the world's most extensive programme of its kind.

---

[1] The Norwegian word *teiknspråk* signifies sign language as opposed to spoken language, but also is the everyday term used for *norsk teiknspråk* (Norwegian Sign Language, NSL). When discussing the legislation I will use the English term *sign language*, in line with the English translation of the Act.

Teachers' competence

As part of the preparations for Reform 97, teachers were offered a half-year full-time training programme in NSL by the government. This was considered sufficient to acquire a basic proficiency to be developed further with practice. The programme represented a considerable effort by the government, but the further development of the teachers' skills was not facilitated everywhere, and ten years later, many hearing teachers in bilingual classrooms still feel their proficiency in NSL is insufficient.

The lack of trained Deaf teachers was addressed by Sør-Trøndelag University College in Trondheim by establishing a specially adapted teacher training programme for Deaf students in 1994. All key positions in the educational system, however, remain filled by hearing professionals, so bilingual deaf education cannot yet be said to be anchored in the Deaf community.

One of the challenges of the introduction of bilingual deaf education, the lack of adequate teaching materials, has been taken seriously by educational authorities. An impressive range of materials based on the new syllabuses has been made available to teachers over the last ten years.

School placement

In principle, section 2-6 of the Act of Education allows parents of deaf children to demand that their local school should offer their child a bilingual programme. Ohna et al. (2003) reported that, by 2002, about one-third of pupils educated according to section 2-6 attended their local school for most of the time. The rest spent most of their time at special schools or units for pupils with hearing loss at the state or municipal level. Since then, the number of full-time pupils in the state-run schools for the deaf has been decreasing. Vonen & Hjulstad (2005) discuss whether this process is making the profession of deaf education weaker and more vulnerable. Recent studies of mainstream classrooms indicate that some pupils experience serious communication inadequacies in interactions with peers (e.g., Ohna et al. 2003, Kermit et al. 2004). The multiple school placements that characterise many pupils also pose pedagogical challenges. More knowledge is needed about the complexities of the classrooms in which deaf pupils are found (Hjulstad & Kristoffersen 2007).

Discourses of cochlear implants

Since the late 1990s, most congenitally deaf children in Norway have received cochlear implants. The surgery is carried out at Rikshospitalet University Hospital in Oslo, and the costs are carried by the health service and social security systems of the government. Referring to the fact that the purpose of the cochlear implant is to give children hearing and the opportunity to develop spoken language communication, the hospital currently recommends, in the default case, that the implanted child should receive auditory verbal/oral education, which will make it possible to acquire approximately normal spoken language skills. For a small group of children who do not, for various reasons, develop spoken language as expected, and for multiply disabled children, the hospital may consider recommending speech with sign support or Sign Language (Siem et al. 2008).

This attitude on the part of the medical institution has evoked much debate. No known research evidence supports the idea that bilingual education hinders spoken language development (Becker & Erlenkamp 2007, Vonen 2007), and the hospital's recommendations could be perceived as contradictory to the government's recognition of NSL as a full language. Similar discourses can be observed even among educators, however, and, according to Hjulstad & Kristoffersen (2007:67), "today's dominant perspective within parts of the field" of deaf education does not include bilingual education. Pushing the situation somewhat, one might accuse some educational counsellors of abandoning their professional role and rather treat parents more or less as "customers" who already have learned from the hospital's implant team what they need. Worries have been expressed about Deaf teachers' future access to classrooms with deaf pupils.

Where are we, and where are we going?

The introduction of the legal right to bilingual education in 1997 must still be considered a landmark event in Norwegian deaf education. Some of the initial challenges have been met in promising ways, such as the teaching material situation and the issue of NSL training for parents. Other challenges still remain: Many hearing teachers' NSL proficiency still is too limited for getting the most out of their pupils' linguistic repertoire. The number of trained Deaf teachers is low, and their leaders are hearing.

The professional controversy concerning language provisions for children with cochlear implants continues to confuse parents, and, clearly, more sincere attempts should be made at improving the professional dialogue. In my view, counselling should be based upon knowledge, genuine respect of both languages and of bilingualism, and an ambition to empower the child himself or herself to make the relevant language choices. Judging by the proud recent history of language rights for deaf children in Norway, I am optimistic about the chances of developing such counselling.

Bibliography

Becker, F & S Erlenkamp (2007): "Et språkløst liv med cochleaimplantat?" [A languageless life with cochlear implants?] *Tidsskrift for Den norske legeforening* 127:2836-2838.

[Education Act] *Act relating to Primary and Secondary Education (Education Act)*. 1998. Last amended 30 June 2000. Online unofficial English translation: http://www.ub.uio.no/ujur/ulovdata/lov-19980717-061-eng.pdf

Hjulstad, O & AE Kristoffersen (2007): "Pupils with a cochlear implant in Norway: perspectives on learning and participation in research and practice." In Hyde, M (ed.) (2007): *To be or to become. Language and learning in young deaf children.* Oslo: Skådalen Resource Centre. 67-90.

Kermit, P, OM Mjøen & A Holm (2005): *Cochleaimplantat i et tospråklig og etisk perspektiv.* [Cochlear implants in a bilingual and ethical perspective.] Trondheim, Norway: Sør-Trøndelag University College.

Ohna, SE, O Hjulstad, AM Vonen, SM Grønlie, E Hjelmervik & G Høie (2003): *På vei mot en ny grunnskoleopplæring for døve elever. En evalueringsstudie etter Reform 97.* [Towards a new compulsory school education for deaf pupils. An evaluation study after Reform 97.] Oslo: Skådalen Resource Centre.

Report to the Storting No. 61 (1984-85): *Om visse sider ved spesialundervisninga og den pedagogisk-psykologiske tenesta* [On certain aspects of special education and the educational-psychological service]. Oslo: Ministry of Education and Church Affairs.

Siem, G, OB Wie & S Harris (2008): "Cochleaimplantat og tegnspråk." [Cochlear implants and Sign Language.] *Tidsskrift for Den norske legeforening* 128.69.

Vonen, AM (2007): "Bilingualism – a future asset in the education of socially deaf children." In Hyde, M & G Høie (eds.): *Constructing educational discourses on deafness*. Oslo: Skådalen Resource Centre. 102-112.

Summary of the conference discussion

For many years Scandinavian countries have been held up as the standard for deaf education. The presentation mentions the right of children to a bilingual education. One delegate asked about the impact of cochlear implants (CIs) on the future of deaf bilingual education.

In Norway, the health service advice on aural/oral education is very different from the advice given by, for example, the Norwegian Association of the Deaf, which is not against cochlear implantation but strongly recommends that children with cochlear implants should be exposed to both languages (Norwegian and Norwegian Sign Language). Advice given by educational counsellors seems to vary, and the parents are the ones to make the perhaps most crucial choices for their child. Many deafness professionals are trying to inform the public and the parents so that their choices can be well-founded. Norwegian Sign Language (NSL) is not yet an endangered language, but if professionals do not reach the decision-makers (including the parents) with information, the language may suffer a new period of marginalisation in society. This is a very sad scenario in the light of the achievements that have been made previously.

In Finland, CIs are considered more of a threat to Finnish Sign Language. The Deaf community in Finland is small, having no more than 5000 Deaf Sign Language users. According to a recent study, more than 90% of Finnish deaf children born since 1997 have received a cochlear implant (until 2007 around 200 children) of whom only 14% use mainly Sign Language, 16% use sign and speech separately and 34% use sign supported speech and the rest (36%) do not sign at all. This means inevitably that the number of 'new arrivals' in the Sign Language community - and future signing parents for their own children - is rapidly reducing in one single generation.

The result has been noted within special education where the number of signing children is declining dramatically: in 2005 43% (versus 21% in the year 2002) of CI children attend mainstream schools instead of schools for the deaf/hard of hearing.

In Norway, CIs and bilingualism can work side-by-side/together, whereas in many countries the two education philosophies are seem as mutually exclusive. However, why should they be? CIs can be great for improving the hearing potential of a person, but that is far from saying that they make the person normally hearing and fully capable of participating in any spoken conversation in situations of any degree of complexity of novelty. So far, it seems that many parents whose children have CIs choose to join the NSL tuition programme. In fact, many of them realise that those weeks when they get together with other parents to learn NSL, are excellent opportunities to get to know the other parents, learn from their experiences and discuss issues of shared interest. In some cases, there is the paradoxical situation that the child is attending an aural/oral programme while the parents are learning NSL.

One view to consider is that CIs are a means to an end - to access sound/speech. The choice of mode of education still depends on all the variables that apply to all Deaf students, with the effectiveness of the CI an additional element. The 'mutually exclusive' stance is so unhelpful and does not represent the true benefits derived from CIs, bilingualism, oral/aural approach, full ASL/BSL/other Sign Language, all of which have significant value to the individuals to whom they are best suited.

In Scotland, virtually all D/deaf children receive implants. The advice from the medical profession does not seem to encourage the use of BSL, and in some cases it is actively discouraged. Medics' (and some special educator's) disregard for Sign Language often comes from a combination of a one-sidedly medical perspective on deafness (i.e., lack of knowledge about the complexity of deafness/Deafhood) and lack of knowledge about the development of language and communication in children. In Australia and the Netherlands a similar situation exists. Parents may be strongly encouraged to stop using all forms of Sign Language and use oral/aural communication only. The assumption seems to be that using Sign Language will stop the development of speech. Sign language is a last resort when speech/listening ability doesn't develop well. There is an irony that 'Babysign' is now being promoted for parents of hearing children to allow them to communicate before speech is developed. So it is encouraged for hearing kids but not deaf or CI children. The research done into 'Babysign' seems to suggest that using Sign Language improves hearing children's vocabulary, spelling ability and IQ among other things. The simultaneous fashions of oralism with implanted children and bilingualism with hearing ones constitutes an interesting paradox.

One aspect to be considered is the terminology used when discussing these matters. Traditionally children with a hearing loss have been divided into two categories - 'deaf' and 'hard-of-hearing'. When bilingual education was introduced, the target group were clearly the 'deaf' children. When 'deaf' children started getting cochlear implants, the idea came up that the implants made the children into a brand new category of children, children 'with CI', distinct from both earlier groups. In this way, the bilingual practices targeted at the deaf children could be put aside as irrelevant for this new group, and even insights from general developmental psychology about the child's active role in his/her own development could be argued to be irrelevant for this very special new group of children that was characterised by an immense need of form-centred speech training. If someone succeed in convincing parents that a child 'with CI' is a totally different thing as compared with a 'deaf' child, then it should be easy to convince them further that Deaf adults' experiences are quite irrelevant to the needs of children with CI. It is important not let category boundaries such as these make us look at these children as if they were different species. We should indeed insist that Sign Language need not be something very exclusive, that its benefits are by no means limited to the most profoundly deaf children. Rather, we should stress that implanted and non-implanted children share that same human need of developing in active and cheerful interaction with their surroundings - and it should be needless to say that those surroundings that are the most accessible to the child's senses are the most important ones.

In the presentation, the author states that "In principle, section 2-6 of the Act of Education allows parents of deaf children to demand that their local school should offer their child a bilingual programme. Ohna et al. (2003) reported that, by 2002, about one-third of pupils educated according to section 2-6 attended their local school for most of the time. The rest spent most of their time at special schools or units for pupils with hearing loss at the state or municipal level.

Since then, the number of full-time pupils in the state-run schools for the deaf has been decreasing." To one delegate it seemed strange that a policy to allow bilingualism should also possibly lead to the closure of many deaf schools. Are there enough professionals to provide all the services, allowed for by the act, for all the deaf children in mainstream schools? The delegate further asked "Does it work in practice, or are the children entitled in theory but given inadequate access in practice?"

It is worth remembering that not all deaf residential schools were successful academic institutions and there was neglect and abuse in some of these schools. Even today, the schools for the deaf in sparsely-populated Norway are small, and they do not seem to be growing. The government reorganised the state-run deaf schools in the early nineties so that they now make up separate departments of resource centres that also offer such services as counselling for teachers in mainstream schools and Sign Language tuition for parents. These centres also receive many mainstreamed children for a few weeks every year as kind of 'language nests' where they can stay and use Norwegian Sign Language in the environment of other signers.

Does bilingual mainstreaming work in practice? In Norwegian classroom studies they have seen classrooms that function astonishingly well, but unfortunately, there have also seen less successful classrooms, as might be expected. In the lower grades at least, it seems that a bilingual programme can work well at least if the child has considerable hearing (e.g., many children with cochlear implants have considerable hearing), if the teachers are reasonably good signers, and if the hearing children in the class are giving the opportunity to learn Norwegian Sign Language (which they usually do with great enthusiasm). Some current research is concerned with documenting the respective roles of the two languages in different bilingual mainstream classrooms. But as we all can imagine, there are also many things that can go wrong, and it is probably right to say that some Norwegian children today have the right to a bilingual education, but are under-resourced.

In the United States there is a lot of mainstreaming with fewer and fewer children attending schools for the Deaf. While this keeps them home, near their families, and may possibly challenge them educationally, their language usually 'deteriorates'. In public schools there are so many people who are not language models, who do not have ASL grammar or structure and who use signed English.

In Norway, since the reform in 1997, lots of teachers have attended Sign Language courses and graduated at university level in Norwegian Sign Language. Also a lot of deaf teachers are educated at the only university level course specially designed for deaf students. So there are a lot of teachers with Sign Language skills that can teach the deaf pupils in the local mainstream school. But is this enough? What kind of Sign Language environment is made by two people? Is this deaf culture?

In Norway, to be a teacher for the deaf you need either an ordinary teacher education certificate (4 years at university level) plus at least half a year full-time elementary training in Norwegian Sign Language from a university or university college, or a particular teacher education certificate (also 4 years) for signers that is offered by the University College in Trondheim. The former option produces many teacher with little Sign Language skills. Graduates from the latter option generally do not work in mainstream schools. Many teachers of the deaf also take courses in special needs education.

In many countries there is concern about the language proficiency (or lack thereof) amongst interpreters in the educational setting, where they may inadvertently end up being the major language model for the Deaf student. While that concern is to be applauded and attending to it is an urgent matter, why does there seem to be no similar worry and action taken to see that teachers of the Deaf have sufficient language skills?

In Norway, in a guiding document published by the Ministry of Education around the time when the bilingual curriculum was introduced in 1997, it was stated very clearly that tuition through the medium of an interpreter is not considered as tuition in Norwegian Sign Language. On the contrary, teachers of deaf children were supposed to be signers themselves. The level of signing skills required was quite low. In classroom studies, nevertheless, it has been seen that the actual communication situation in the classroom with one deaf and many hearing pupils sometimes is indistinguishable from an interpreter-mediated situation, except that the 'interpreter' is a teacher with limited signing skills and without the interpreter's code of ethics concerning his/her role in the communication. All this said, it is no secret that a number of mainstream classrooms today simply do not obey the definition of bilingual education in the Ministry's 1997 statement (it seems simply to have been forgotten by many in the practice field) and do engage regular professional interpreters (who tend to be better signers but have no educational training and whose code of ethics was not constructed with an eye of the classroom as the prototypical arena).

Index

accommodation, 25, 30, 81
administrators, 14, 25, 26, 118, 140, 141, 145, 148, 149, 152, 153, 154, 155, 156, 157, 159, 160
amplification, 17, 37
articulation, 48, 157
ASL, 27, 28, 29, 32, 34, 37, 38, 39, 40, 50, 52, 53, 56, 69, 70, 75, 88, 89, 90, 91, 92, 93, 94, 95, 96, 97, 98, 99, 100, 101, 102, 103, 104, 105, 106, 107, 112, 117, 118, 124, 127, 129, 131, 132, 133, 134, 136, 161, 171, 174
auditory skills, 27
autonomy, 14
Babysign, 171
background knowledge, 57, 133, 161
behavioural modification, 31
bicultural, 61, 82, 101
bilingual, 35, 61, 80, 82, 101, 157, 164, 165, 166, 167, 168, 170, 172, 173, 174
bilingualism, 45, 104, 168, 171, 172, 173
boundaries, 70, 71, 72, 73, 74, 76, 78, 80, 81, 82, 83, 103, 106, 112, 113, 159, 172
boundary, 70, 71, 72, 73, 74, 76, 79, 81, 82
BSL, 63, 64, 171
certification, 100, 108, 111, 113, 114, 115, 122, 123, 137, 149, 154

certified interpreters, 111, 115, 116
Children of Deaf Adults, 72
clarification techniques, 32
classifiers, 92, 132, 136
classroom, 6, 7, 8, 9, 10, 11, 12, 13, 14, 15, 16, 19, 20, 23, 25, 26, 28, 29, 32, 46, 47, 51, 52, 53, 54, 56, 58, 59, 61, 63, 66, 68, 69, 70, 71, 72, 73, 74, 75, 77, 78, 80, 81, 82, 84, 86, 87, 88, 89, 90, 92, 95, 102, 108, 109, 110, 111, 122, 123, 124, 125, 126, 127, 130, 135, 137, 142, 143, 144, 145, 147, 149, 150, 152, 153, 154, 155, 156, 157, 160, 161, 162, 173, 174
clause, 98, 106, 107
cochlear implant, 57, 167, 168, 170
cochlear implants, 10, 17, 18, 21, 26, 27, 35, 53, 57, 66, 167, 168, 170, 172, 173
CODA, 72
code of ethics, 22, 46, 175
Code of Professional Conduct, 35, 39, 74, 79, 108
cognition, 10, 12, 17, 19, 21, 22, 51, 58, 59, 60, 101, 121
cognitive development, 8, 19, 22, 55, 66, 99
cognitive overload, 93
cognitive strategies, 51
cohesion, 93, 110
communication breakdown, 49
communication flexibility, 68

communicative goals, 89
comprehension, 10, 11, 18, 19, 48, 51, 55, 56, 59, 62, 65, 111, 134
Comprehension, 21, 61, 86, 110, 111
conceptualisation, 7
conditional, 97, 98, 106, 107
conduit, 13, 15, 27, 82
confidentiality, 14
context, 9, 21, 22, 27, 34, 55, 58, 80, 95, 101, 103, 120, 137, 143, 156, 159
conversation, 13, 33, 77, 81, 86, 95, 103, 122, 134, 135, 142, 171
critical thinking skills, 86, 120
cues, 88, 129
curriculum, 29, 51, 60, 108, 161, 165, 174
Deaf community, 33, 46, 91, 115, 166, 170
Deaf consumer, 72, 76, 77
Deaf consumers, 71, 72, 76, 111
Deaf culture, 28, 33, 37, 152
deaf families, 10
deaf parents, 10, 55, 57, 66, 123, 132
Deaf school, 30, 42
Deaf voice, 35
Demand-Control schema, 119
direct versus interpreted communication, 10
discourse, 6, 15, 16, 18, 20, 22, 23, 26, 88, 89, 92, 93, 94, 95, 97, 100, 103, 104, 107, 109, 110, 161, 164
disfluency, 118
educational interpreter, 7, 8, 14, 15, 17, 26, 69, 74, 97, 99, 100, 107, 122, 136

Educational Interpreter Performance Assessment, 7, 87, 108
educational interpreters, 5, 7, 8, 9, 11, 13, 14, 15, 17, 19, 22, 23, 24, 26, 27, 46, 71, 72, 81, 87, 88, 90, 91, 97, 99, 104, 107, 115, 116, 137, 144, 150
educational teams, 14, 16
EIPA, 8, 13, 22, 104, 107, 108, 109, 115, 122
Elementary and Secondary Education Act, 84, 85
emphasis, 35, 45, 53, 120, 134
empirical evidence, 16
empowerment, 81
English as a second language, 64
English-based sign systems, 27
ESEA, 84, 85
ethical decision-making, 120
expression, 67, 92, 101, 103, 110
expressive sign skills, 45
extralinguistic knowledge, 93
eye gaze, 80, 102, 107, 134
eyebrows, 106, 118
facial expressions, 28, 72, 97
feedback, 69, 75, 120, 147, 152, 161
fingerspelled, 31, 40, 66
fingerspelling, 66, 109, 145, 148
flexibility, 70, 82
fluency, 8, 88, 89, 90, 91, 95, 109, 118
formal register, 36
functional speech, 9, 26, 27
genre, 89
grammar, 31, 64, 66, 89, 90, 94, 95, 108, 109, 112, 174
group discussions, 13, 143, 157, 160

handshape, 40, 112
hard-of-hearing, 22, 24, 26, 35, 60, 61, 87, 104, 141, 172
hearing aids, 17, 21, 136
hearing consumers, 111
hearing loss, 9, 10, 53, 55, 56, 62, 166, 172
hearing parents, 9, 10, 53, 57, 65, 66
hearing peers, 10, 11, 12, 52, 54, 55, 56, 57, 68, 86, 140, 147, 148, 149, 156
IEP, 9, 15, 75
illusion of inclusion, 25, 141, 154
imperative, 95
incidental learning, 65, 159
inclusion, 25, 68, 69, 84, 105, 140, 150, 154, 155, 156, 159
inclusive education model, 140, 156
Individual Educational Plans, 81
inference, 67
inferences, 55, 97, 99
inflection, 35, 113
intelligibility, 93
intelligible output, 86
interpretation, 6, 7, 8, 11, 13, 15, 16, 25, 28, 29, 30, 31, 32, 33, 34, 35, 36, 45, 47, 48, 53, 64, 81, 82, 84, 86, 87, 88, 89, 92, 93, 100, 103, 112, 115, 118, 122, 125, 127, 129, 133, 134, 136, 140, 143, 145, 146, 147, 148, 149, 153, 154, 156, 161
interpreted education, 6, 9, 10, 12, 13, 16, 19, 20, 22, 25, 87, 105
Interpreter Training Program, 108
interruptions, 50
intonation, 31, 48, 89, 93, 102, 108

irony, 89, 99, 171
ITPs, 45, 116
K-12, 6, 8, 10, 14, 16, 19, 28, 104
language acquisition, 66, 90, 93, 101, 102, 104
language fluency, 86, 100
learning styles, 54
least restrictive environment', 159
lexical items, 97
lexicon, 36, 60
linguistic appropriateness, 37
linguistic competence, 97
linguistic isolation, 159
literacy, 8, 17, 20, 55, 56, 57, 58, 59, 61, 62, 67, 85, 86, 117, 157
mainstream, 18, 24, 45, 47, 51, 52, 61, 63, 84, 87, 154, 159, 166, 170, 173, 174, 175
mainstreaming, 25, 26, 68, 159, 173
manually coded English, 27
meaning, 34, 37, 48, 55, 60, 66, 67, 89, 91, 92, 93, 94, 95, 99, 105, 112, 113, 122, 135
meaningful communication, 86
mediated education, 140, 141, 159
mentoring, 119, 138, 160
metacognition, 7, 11, 67, 161
metacognitive skills, 7, 25, 161
misunderstanding, 32, 35, 89
modality, 54, 56, 57, 65, 84, 90
morphological, 49
name signs, 47
narration, 48, 49
National Association of the Deaf, 74
NCLB, 84, 85, 86
neutrality, 14, 102
No Child Left Behind, 84, 86

non-manual grammatical features, 91
non-manual marker, 97, 107
non-manual markers, 97, 110, 111, 117
Non-manual markers, 91
non-manual signals, 93, 97
non-native signers, 37
nonsense, 48, 49
Norwegian Sign Language, 164, 165, 170, 173, 174
NSL, 164, 165, 166, 167, 168, 170, 171
omissions, 7, 8, 11, 21, 86, 87, 94, 103, 112
oral communication, 27
parameters, 112, 149
para-pro, 69, 76
paraprofessional, 69
pedagogy, 51
phonics, 31
phonological, 49, 59, 104
physical space, 80
policies, 15, 28, 29, 151
pragmatics, 97
preferred language, 57
prep time, 36, 125
preparation, 7, 23, 50, 54, 55, 116, 122, 125, 136, 161
prepositions, 92
primary language, 64
professionalism, 144
profound hearing loss, 17
pronoun, 94
prosody, 90, 93, 97, 100, 102, 104, 105, 108, 109, 110
public schools, 21, 49, 81, 86, 103, 104, 174
punctuation, 30, 31, 48
Qualifications, 8, 49, 88
qualified interpreters, 140, 142, 151, 156

rapport, 70, 73, 82
reading, 10, 18, 19, 21, 29, 32, 46, 48, 55, 56, 57, 58, 59, 61, 62, 65, 78, 85, 88, 100, 161
receptive skills, 45, 46
register, 35, 47, 94, 112
Registry of Interpreters for the Deaf, 22, 23, 24, 35, 39, 74, 79, 105, 108, 139
regulations, 15
rhetorical questions, 95, 99
RID, 23, 35, 39, 79, 100, 108, 111, 113, 114, 115, 116, 139
sarcasm, 89
second language users, 68
second-language learners, 11, 87
SEE, 42, 124, 129, 131, 132, 133, 136, 145
self-esteem, 81, 147, 154, 155
semantic intent, 34, 46
sight lines, 80, 81
Sign Language, 10, 18, 19, 20, 21, 27, 28, 33, 47, 49, 53, 54, 55, 56, 57, 58, 59, 61, 62, 63, 64, 65, 66, 69, 79, 84, 88, 92, 100, 101, 102, 103, 104, 105, 108, 117, 124, 127, 138, 140, 141, 145, 157, 158, 164, 165, 167, 169, 170, 171, 172, 173, 174
Sign Language community, 170
sign production, 31, 36, 46, 95, 109, 110
sign systems, 118
signed English, 112, 117, 174
Signed Exact English, 49, 145
signing style, 46
signing system, 49
sign-to-voice, 111
social accessibility, 13, 26

social isolation, 140, 147, 159
socialisation, 67
sociolinguistic, 18, 34, 103
source language, 93, 94, 112, 113
source message, 48, 94
special education, 27, 84, 169, 170
special educators, 14
spoken communication, 17
spoken English, 45, 56, 69, 88
spoken language, 28, 47, 53, 54, 55, 56, 57, 66, 90, 93, 165, 167
stakeholders, 24, 29, 32, 33, 71, 157, 159
standards, 7, 13, 15, 22, 24, 73, 74, 76, 78, 81, 82, 84, 85, 87, 107, 108, 117, 136, 141
suffix, 49
target language, 45, 93, 94, 112
teacher of the Deaf, 33, 78
Theory of Mind, 20, 67, 99, 115
Thought Worlds, 126, 137

translation, 9, 14, 23, 29, 31, 34, 40, 49, 70, 89, 93, 98, 102, 110, 111, 165, 168
transliteration, 53, 56, 112
turn-taking, 15, 111
utterance, 34
visual demands, 127, 133
visual representation, 91, 92
visual stress, 81
visual-spatial language, 26
vocabulary, 7, 8, 10, 11, 27, 32, 35, 46, 50, 55, 59, 65, 66, 94, 99, 109, 110, 111, 120, 127, 128, 131, 133, 172
voice, 29, 34, 35, 36, 45, 46, 48, 50, 52, 108, 111, 112
voicing, 28, 30, 34, 35, 37, 45, 46, 47, 77
Vygotsky, 25, 31
wh-question, 98, 107
word knowledge, 55, 65
word-for-word voicing, 34
Zone of Proximal Development, 31